KB275856

혼공

중학 영문법 마스터

Level 3

혼공북스

이 책의 구성과 특징

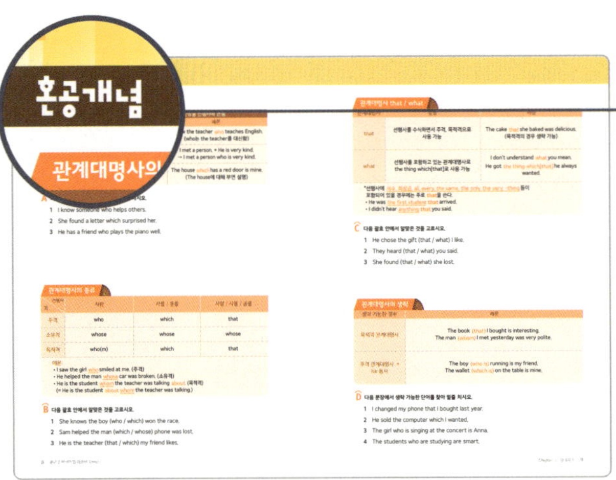

1 문법 개념 확인

문법 설명에서 꼭 배워야 할 핵심 내용을 도표로 정리했습니다. 각 개념을 배운 후에는 연계 문제를 통해 복습할 수 있습니다.

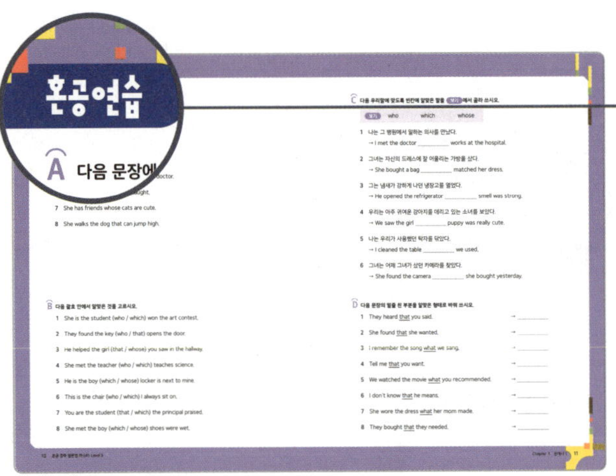

2 학습한 문법 내용 적용

'혼공개념'에서 학습한 문법에 대한 이해도를 점검할 수 있는 문제로 구성했습니다. 가장 기초적인 연습 문제를 통해 학습한 개념을 바로 확인해 볼 수 있습니다.

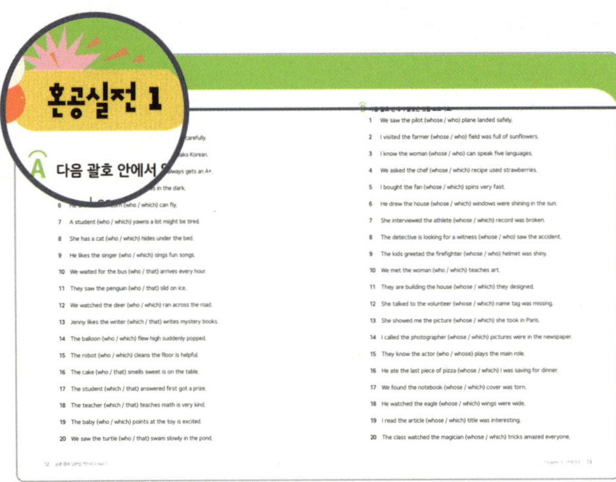

3 대표 기출 유형 연습

'혼공연습'에서 한 걸음 나아간 문제로 구성했습니다. 학습한 문법 개념들을 본격적으로 적용해 볼 수 있는 단계별 문제를 통해, 개념을 정확하게 이해할 수 있도록 구성했습니다.

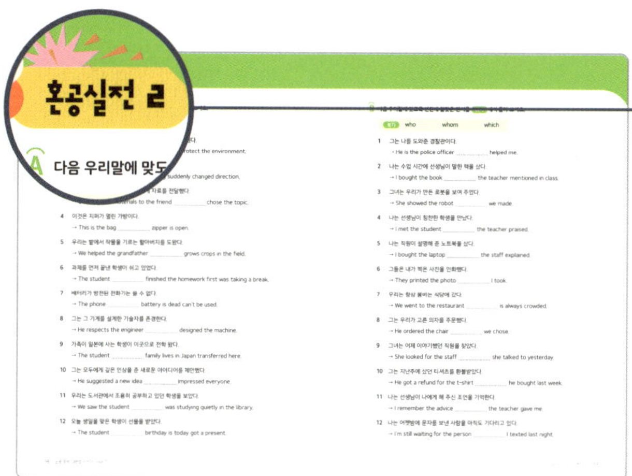

4 서술형 평가 완성

서술형 평가에 대비할 수 있도록 빈칸에 알맞은 단어를 채우고, 문장을 영작할 수 있는 문제로 구성했습니다. 문법 개념을 이해하는 것뿐 아니라 쓰기에서도 활용하며 확실히 습득할 수 있습니다.

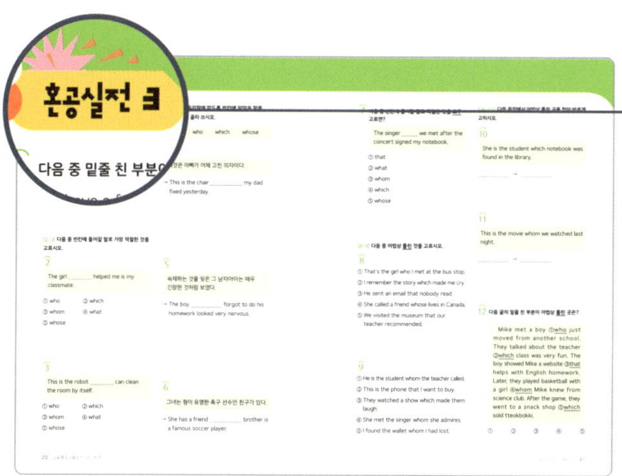

5 학교 시험 완벽 대비

각 챕터에서 배운 내용을 바탕으로 객관식, 주관식, 서술형, 독해 문제를 구성했습니다. 문제를 풀며 자신의 강점과 약점을 스스로 평가하고 학교 시험 실전 감각을 키울 수 있습니다.

400만 명의 수강생이 선택한 EBS 인기 강사 혼공쌤의 강의 32강을 무료로 수강할 수 있습니다.

유쾌한 혼공쌤의 강의를 통해 진정한 **중학 영문법 마스터**가 되어 보세요!

차례

관계사 1

- 관계대명사의 역할
- 관계대명사의 종류
- 관계대명사 that / what
- 관계대명사의 생략

관계대명사의 역할

앞에 나온 명사(선행사)를 대신하면서, 뒤에 오는 문장을 선행사에 연결		
역할	설명	예문
대명사	앞에 나온 명사(선행사)를 대신함	I know the teacher who teaches English. (who는 the teacher를 대신함)
접속사	두 문장을 연결	I met a person. + He is very kind. → I met a person who is very kind.
형용사	앞에 오는 명사를 꾸밈	The house which has a red door is mine. (The house에 대해 부연 설명)

A 다음 문장에서 관계대명사를 찾아 밑줄 치시오.

1　I know someone who helps others.

2　She found a letter which surprised her.

3　He has a friend who plays the piano well.

관계대명사의 종류

격 \ 선행사	사람	사물 / 동물	사람 / 사물 / 동물
주격	who	which	that
소유격	whose	whose	whose
목적격	who(m)	which	that

예문:
- I saw the girl who smiled at me. (주격)
- He helped the man whose car was broken. (소유격)
- He is the student whom the teacher was talking about. (목적격)
  (= He is the student about whom the teacher was talking.)

B 다음 괄호 안에서 알맞은 것을 고르시오.

1　She knows the boy (who / which) won the race.

2　Sam helped the man (which / whose) phone was lost.

3　He is the teacher (that / which) my friend likes.

관계대명사	설명	예문
that	선행사를 수식하면서 주격, 목적격으로 사용 가능	The cake that she baked was delicious. (목적격의 경우 생략 가능)
what	선행사를 포함하고 있는 관계대명사로 the thing which[that]로 사용 가능	I don't understand what you mean. He got the thing which[that] he always wanted.

*선행사에 서수, 최상급, all, every, the same, the only, the very, -thing 등이 포함되어 있을 경우에는 주로 **that**을 쓴다.
• He was the first student **that** arrived.
• I didn't hear anything **that** you said.

C 다음 괄호 안에서 알맞은 것을 고르시오.

1 He chose the gift (that / what) I like.

2 They heard (that / what) you said.

3 She found (that / what) she lost.

관계대명사의 생략

생략 가능한 경우	예문
목적격 관계대명사	The book (that) I bought is interesting. The man (whom) I met yesterday was very polite.
주격 관계대명사 + be 동사	The boy (who is) running is my friend. The wallet (which is) on the table is mine.

D 다음 문장에서 생략 가능한 단어를 찾아 밑줄 치시오.

1 I changed my phone that I bought last year.

2 He sold the computer which I wanted.

3 The girl who is singing at the concert is Anna.

4 The students who are studying are smart.

A 다음 문장에서 관계대명사를 찾아 밑줄 치시오.

1 I know the boy who runs fast.

2 I saw the man who helps animals.

3 Amy is the girl who likes soccer.

4 You saw the movie which I like.

5 He talked to the man whose son is a doctor.

6 You helped the girl whom I taught.

7 She has friends whose cats are cute.

8 She walks the dog that can jump high.

B 다음 괄호 안에서 알맞은 것을 고르시오.

1 She is the student (who / which) won the art contest.

2 They found the key (who / that) opens the door.

3 He helped the girl (that / whose) you saw in the hallway.

4 She met the teacher (who / which) teaches science.

5 He is the boy (which / whose) locker is next to mine.

6 This is the chair (who / which) I always sit on.

7 You are the student (that / which) the principal praised.

8 She met the boy (which / whose) shoes were wet.

C 다음 우리말에 맞도록 빈칸에 알맞은 말을 보기 에서 골라 쓰시오.

보기   who   which   whose

1   나는 그 병원에서 일하는 의사를 만났다.

→ I met the doctor ____________ works at the hospital.

2   그녀는 자신의 드레스에 잘 어울리는 가방을 샀다.

→ She bought a bag ____________ matched her dress.

3   그는 냄새가 강하게 나던 냉장고를 열었다.

→ He opened the refrigerator ____________ smell was strong.

4   우리는 아주 귀여운 강아지를 데리고 있는 소녀를 보았다.

→ We saw the girl ____________ puppy was really cute.

5   나는 우리가 사용했던 탁자를 닦았다.

→ I cleaned the table ____________ we used.

6   그녀는 어제 그녀가 샀던 카메라를 찾았다.

→ She found the camera ____________ she bought yesterday.

D 다음 문장의 밑줄 친 부분을 알맞은 형태로 바꿔 쓰시오.

1   They heard <u>that</u> you said.   → ____________

2   She found <u>that</u> she wanted.   → ____________

3   I remember the song <u>what</u> we sang.   → ____________

4   Tell me <u>that</u> you want.   → ____________

5   We watched the movie <u>what</u> you recommended.   → ____________

6   I don't know <u>that</u> he means.   → ____________

7   She wore the dress <u>what</u> her mom made.   → ____________

8   They bought <u>that</u> they needed.   → ____________

A 다음 괄호 안에서 알맞은 것을 고르시오.

1   I saw the girl (who / which) was running quickly.

2   She talked to the nurse (who / which) listens carefully.

3   My dad called the doctor (who / which) speaks Korean.

4   They know the student (who / which) always gets an A+.

5   I saw the fish (who / which) glows in the dark.

6   He drew the unicorn (who / which) can fly.

7   A student (who / which) yawns a lot might be tired.

8   She has a cat (who / which) hides under the bed.

9   He likes the singer (who / which) sings fun songs.

10   We waited for the bus (who / that) arrives every hour.

11   They saw the penguin (who / that) slid on ice.

12   We watched the deer (who / which) ran across the road.

13   Jenny likes the writer (which / that) writes mystery books.

14   The balloon (who / which) flew high suddenly popped.

15   The robot (who / which) cleans the floor is helpful.

16   The cake (who / that) smells sweet is on the table.

17   The student (which / that) answered first got a prize.

18   The teacher (which / that) teaches math is very kind.

19   The baby (who / which) points at the toy is excited.

20   We saw the turtle (who / that) swam slowly in the pond.

B 다음 괄호 안에서 알맞은 것을 고르시오.

1   We saw the pilot (whose / who) plane landed safely.

2   I visited the farmer (whose / who) field was full of sunflowers.

3   I know the woman (whose / who) can speak five languages.

4   We asked the chef (whose / which) recipe used strawberries.

5   I bought the fan (whose / which) spins very fast.

6   He drew the house (whose / which) windows were shining in the sun.

7   She interviewed the athlete (whose / which) record was broken.

8   The detective is looking for a witness (whose / who) saw the accident.

9   The kids greeted the firefighter (whose / who) helmet was shiny.

10   We met the woman (who / which) teaches art.

11   They are building the house (whose / which) they designed.

12   She talked to the volunteer (whose / which) name tag was missing.

13   She showed me the picture (whose / which) she took in Paris.

14   I called the photographer (whose / which) pictures were in the newspaper.

15   They know the actor (who / whose) plays the main role.

16   He ate the last piece of pizza (whose / which) I was saving for dinner.

17   We found the notebook (whose / which) cover was torn.

18   He watched the eagle (whose / which) wings were wide.

19   I read the article (whose / which) title was interesting.

20   The class watched the magician (whose / which) tricks amazed everyone.

C 다음 괄호 안에서 알맞은 것을 고르시오.

1 She's the friend (whom / which) I invited to the party.

2 She painted the wall (whom / which) we saw yesterday.

3 I lost the ticket (whom / which) I bought this morning.

4 The woman (whom / whose) I called didn't answer.

5 We cleaned the bench (whom / which) the kids used.

6 He ate the sandwich (whom / which) his mom made.

7 They fixed the machine (who / which) we borrowed.

8 The person (who / which) you mentioned is my uncle.

9 She opened the box (that / whose) her teacher gave.

10 The boy (whom / which) they chose was very talented.

11 He returned the book (that / whose) I lent him.

12 We watered the plant (that / whom) our friend sent us.

13 He loved the dog (that / whose) they adopted.

14 She chose the dress (that / whom) her sister recommended.

15 He counted the coins (which / whose) his friend dropped.

16 I remember the song (that / whom) we sang last year.

17 We followed the path (whom / which) the guide suggested.

18 They borrowed the board game (that / who) the teacher brought.

19 He saved the video (who / which) his class made.

20 I returned the umbrella (who / which) you left here.

D 다음 대화의 괄호 안에서 알맞은 것을 고르시오.

1 A: Did you hear (what / that) she said at the meeting?
  B: Yes, it was really surprising.

2 A: Can you bring (what / that) you bought from the bookstore?
  B: Sure. I have it in my locker.

3 A: Is this the movie (what / that) you watched at the theater?
  B: Yes! I watched it with my cousin.

4 A: I couldn't hear (what / that) the GPS said.
  B: It told you to turn right.

5 A: That's the store (what / that) sells the cute backpacks, right?
  B: Yes! Let's go check them out.

6 A: Can you hand me (what / that) I need to make the omelet?
  B: Sure, here are some eggs and a pan.

7 A: I didn't understand (what / that) the teacher explained in class.
  B: Me neither. Let's study about it together.

8 A: That's the jacket (what / that) I wanted to buy last week.
  B: It's on sale today. Let's get one!

9 A: I forgot (what / that) we need for the science project.
  B: Don't worry. I wrote it down.

10 A: Is this the restaurant (what / that) you recommended?
   B: Yes! Their pasta is amazing.

A 다음 우리말에 맞도록 빈칸에 알맞은 단어를 보기 에서 골라 쓰시오.

보기   who   which   whose

1 우리는 환경을 보호하는 데 도움이 되는 방법을 배웠다.

→ We learned ways ___________ help us protect the environment.

2 운전 중이던 남자가 갑자기 방향을 틀었다.

→ The man ___________ was driving suddenly changed direction.

3 그녀는 그 주제를 선택한 친구에게 자료를 전달했다.

→ She sent the materials to the friend ___________ chose the topic.

4 이것은 지퍼가 열린 가방이다.

→ This is the bag ___________ zipper is open.

5 우리는 밭에서 작물을 기르는 할아버지를 도왔다.

→ We helped the grandfather ___________ grows crops in the field.

6 과제를 먼저 끝낸 학생이 쉬고 있었다.

→ The student ___________ finished the homework first was taking a break.

7 배터리가 방전된 전화기는 쓸 수 없다.

→ The phone ___________ battery is dead can't be used.

8 그는 그 기계를 설계한 기술자를 존경한다.

→ He respects the engineer ___________ designed the machine.

9 가족이 일본에 사는 학생이 이곳으로 전학 왔다.

→ The student ___________ family lives in Japan transferred here.

10 그는 모두에게 깊은 인상을 준 새로운 아이디어를 제안했다.

→ He suggested a new idea ___________ impressed everyone.

11 우리는 도서관에서 조용히 공부하고 있던 학생을 보았다.

→ We saw the student ___________ was studying quietly in the library.

12 오늘 생일을 맞은 학생이 선물을 받았다.

→ The student ___________ birthday is today got a present.

보기　who　　　whom　　　which

1 그는 나를 도와준 경찰관이다.

→ He is the police officer ___________ helped me.

2 나는 수업 시간에 선생님이 말한 책을 샀다.

→ I bought the book ___________ the teacher mentioned in class.

3 그녀는 우리가 만든 로봇을 보여 주었다.

→ She showed the robot ___________ we made.

4 나는 선생님이 칭찬한 학생을 만났다.

→ I met the student ___________ the teacher praised.

5 나는 직원이 설명해 준 노트북을 샀다.

→ I bought the laptop ___________ the staff explained.

6 그들은 내가 찍은 사진을 인화했다.

→ They printed the photo ___________ I took.

7 우리는 항상 붐비는 식당에 갔다.

→ We went to the restaurant ___________ is always crowded.

8 그는 우리가 고른 의자를 주문했다.

→ He ordered the chair ___________ we chose.

9 그녀는 어제 이야기했던 직원을 찾았다.

→ She looked for the staff ___________ she talked to yesterday.

10 그는 지난주에 샀던 티셔츠를 환불받았다.

→ He got a refund for the t-shirt ___________ he bought last week.

11 나는 선생님이 나에게 해 주신 조언을 기억한다.

→ I remember the advice ___________ the teacher gave me.

12 나는 어젯밤에 문자를 보낸 사람을 아직도 기다리고 있다.

→ I'm still waiting for the person ___________ I texted last night.

C 다음 우리말에 맞도록 괄호 안의 단어들을 바르게 배열하시오.

1 나는 나를 도와준 소녀를 기억한다.
(remember / me / I / the girl / helped / who / .)

→ ____

2 그녀는 공을 차는 선수를 인터뷰했다.
(the ball / interviewed / she / the player / kicks / who / .)

→ ____

3 나는 소리를 녹음하는 앱을 발견했다.
(found / I / which / sound / the app / records / .)

→ ____

4 나는 자전거를 도둑맞은 한 소년을 만났다.
(a boy / met / bike / stolen / I / whose / was / .)

→ ____

5 그는 움직임을 감지하는 카메라를 설치했다.
(which / the camera / installed / detects movement / he / .)

→ ____

6 나는 배터리가 방전된 스마트워치를 발견했다.
(I / whose / found / the smartwatch / battery / dead / was / .)

→ ____

7 그는 모두가 신뢰하는 리더다.
(is / he / everyone / whom / the leader / trusts / .)

→ ____

8 그녀는 내가 만났던 친구에게 편지를 보냈다.
(sent / she / a letter / to the friend / met / I / whom / .)

→ ____

9 우리는 우리가 사용한 도구들을 치웠다.
(cleaned up / which / the tools / we used / we / .)

→ ____

10 그는 선생님이 설명한 규칙을 이해했다.
(he / the rule / understood / that / explained / the teacher / .)

→ ____

 다음 우리말에 맞도록 괄호 안의 단어들을 바르게 배열하시오.

1 그녀는 내가 좋아하는 노래를 불렀다.
(that / sang / like / the song / she / I / .)

→ _______________________________________

2 그는 자신이 한 말에 대해 후회했다.
(he / what / said / regretted / he / .)

→ _______________________________________

3 너는 내가 했던 것을 기억하니?
(remember / did / I / what / you / do / ?)

→ _______________________________________

4 나는 그가 쓴 시를 읽었다.
(he / that / read / wrote / I / the poem / .)

→ _______________________________________

5 너는 내가 본 것을 믿지 못할 것이다.
(you / what / won't / saw / I / believe / .)

→ _______________________________________

6 우리는 네가 보여 준 것을 따라 했다.
(we / what / followed / showed / you / .)

→ _______________________________________

7 나는 그녀가 나에게 준 것이 무엇인지 몰랐다.
(gave / she / I / what / didn't / me / know / .)

→ _______________________________________

8 나는 친구가 연주한 것을 녹음했다.
(what / played / recorded / I / my friend / .)

→ _______________________________________

9 그는 그녀가 원하는 모든 것을 사 줬다.
(he / that / bought / everything / wanted / she / .)

→ _______________________________________

10 그는 내가 보낸 이메일을 삭제했다.
(I / he / sent / the email / deleted / .)

→ _______________________________________

1 다음 중 밑줄 친 부분이 어법상 **틀린** 것은?

① I have a friend <u>who</u> lives in Busan.

② She likes stories <u>which</u> have happy endings.

③ He made a cake <u>which</u> looks delicious.

④ She bought a laptop <u>who</u> is very light and fast.

⑤ She thanked the man <u>who</u> found her lost wallet.

[2-3] 다음 중 빈칸에 들어갈 말로 가장 적절한 것을 고르시오.

2

The girl _________ helped me is my classmate.

① who   ② which

③ whom   ④ what

⑤ whose

3

This is the robot _________ can clean the room by itself.

① who   ② which

③ whom   ④ what

⑤ whose

[4-6] 다음 우리말에 맞도록 빈칸에 알맞은 말을 **보기** 에서 골라 쓰시오.

보기   who   which   whose

4

이것은 아빠가 어제 고친 의자이다.

→ This is the chair ___________ my dad fixed yesterday.

5

숙제하는 것을 잊은 그 남자아이는 매우 긴장한 것처럼 보였다.

→ The boy ___________ forgot to do his homework looked very nervous.

6

그녀는 형이 유명한 축구 선수인 친구가 있다.

→ She has a friend ___________ brother is a famous soccer player.

7 다음 중 빈칸에 들어갈 말로 적절한 것을 <u>모두</u> 고르면?

The singer ______ we met after the concert signed my notebook.

① that

② what

③ whom

④ which

⑤ whose

[8-9] 다음 중 어법상 <u>틀린</u> 것을 고르시오.

8

① That's the girl who I met at the bus stop.

② I remember the story which made me cry.

③ He sent an email that nobody read.

④ She called a friend whose lives in Canada.

⑤ We visited the museum that our teacher recommended.

9

① He is the student whom the teacher called.

② This is the phone that I want to buy.

③ They watched a show which made them laugh.

④ She met the singer whom she admires.

⑤ I found the wallet whom I had lost.

[10-11] 다음 문장에서 어법상 <u>틀린</u> 곳을 찾아 바르게 고치시오.

10

She is the student which notebook was found in the library.

____________ → ____________

11

This is the movie whom we watched last night.

____________ → ____________

12 다음 글의 밑줄 친 부분이 어법상 <u>틀린</u> 곳은?

Mike met a boy ①<u>who</u> just moved from another school. They talked about the teacher ②<u>which</u> class was very fun. The boy showed Mike a website ③<u>that</u> helps with English homework. Later, they played basketball with a girl ④<u>whom</u> Mike knew from science club. After the game, they went to a snack shop ⑤<u>which</u> sold tteokbokki.

①   ②   ③   ④   ⑤

[13-14] 다음 빈칸에 공통으로 들어갈 말로 가장 적절한 것을 고르시오.

13

- I didn't understand _______ she meant.
- He wrote down _______ he heard in class.

① who ② that

③ what ④ whom

⑤ which

14

- The girl _______ sits next to me is very friendly.
- I like the movie _______ you recommended last week.

① who ② that

③ what ④ whom

⑤ which

[15-18] 다음 우리말에 맞도록 빈칸에 알맞은 말을 쓰시오.

15

나는 세 가지 악기를 연주할 수 있는 소년을 안다.

→ I know a boy _________ can play three instruments.

16

그녀는 어제 산 가방을 나에게 보여 주었다.

→ She showed me the bag _________ she bought yesterday.

17

그는 발견으로 세상을 바꾼 과학자이다.

→ He is the scientist _________ discovery changed the world.

18

그는 박물관에서 본 것을 믿을 수 없었다.

→ He couldn't believe _________ he saw at the museum.

19

A: Who is the speaker?
B: He's the author _______ books became bestsellers.

① who
② what
③ whom
④ which
⑤ whose

20

A: Who are those students near the door?
B: They're the kids _______ our teacher asked to come.

① what
② whom
③ them
④ which
⑤ whose

21 다음 우리말에 맞도록 괄호 안의 단어들을 바르게 배열하시오.

나는 네가 좋아하는 책을 읽었어.
(read / that / I / the book / like / you / .)

→ ________________________________

22 다음 두 대화의 빈칸에 들어갈 말이 바르게 짝지어진 것은?

• A: I wrote down _______ I needed to pack for the trip.
  B: That's a good idea.
• A: Who's that boy?
  B: He's the student _______ jacket was left in the gym.

① what - whose
② which - whose
③ what - who
④ that - whom
⑤ who - what

23 다음 글의 밑줄 친 부분 중 어법상 옳은 것끼리 바르게 짝지어진 것은?

I have a cousin ⓐwho lives in Jeju. He has a dog ⓑthat loves to swim in the sea. We often visit the cousin ⓒwho house is near the beach. We thanked his sister ⓓwhose cookies were delicious. He also showed me a book ⓔwhat he wrote about his travels.

① ⓐ, ⓑ
② ⓑ, ⓒ
③ ⓑ, ⓓ
④ ⓐ, ⓑ, ⓓ
⑤ ⓑ, ⓓ, ⓔ

CHAPTER

2

관계사 2

- 관계대명사의 계속적 용법
- 관계부사
- 복합관계대명사
- 복합관계부사

관계대명사의 계속적 용법

개념	관계대명사 앞에 반드시 콤마(,) 사용 선행사에 대한 부가적인 설명 *that은 사용 불가 예문: She has a brother, who lives in Canada.	
역할	**접속사 + 대명사** 예문: He saw three lions, which (= and they) were sleeping under a tree.	**앞 문장 전체를 선행사로 받는 경우** 예문: He forgot his homework, which (= and it) surprised the teacher.

A 다음 문장에서 관계대명사 which로 바꿔 쓸 수 있는 부분을 찾아 밑줄 치시오.

1 We saw many paintings, and they impressed us.

2 He missed the bus, and it made him late for school.

관계부사

	접속사 + 부사의 역할을 하면서 선행사를 수식		
	선행사 예시	관계부사	전치사 + 관계대명사
시간	the time, the day, the year	when	in / at / on / during + which
장소	the place, the city, the country	where	in / at / on / to + which
이유	the reason	why	for which
방법	the way	how	in / by + which

예문:
- I still think about the time when(= at which) we went on a trip together.
- That is the place where(= at which) we took a group photo.
- I like the way[how] he speaks. (the way와 how는 함께 사용 불가)

선행사/ 관계부사 생략	선행사가 일반적인 시간, 장소, 이유(time, place, reason)일 때 관계부사나 선행사 중 하나 생략 가능 예시: the time when = the time 또는 when

B 다음 괄호 안에서 알맞은 것을 고르시오.

1 I remember the time (when / where) we first met at the market.

2 This is the place (what / where) I bought my school bag.

3 I don't know the reason (why / how) he is angry.

복합관계대명사

복합관계대명사	명사절	양보 부사절
	「관계대명사 + ever」의 형태로 명사절 또는 부사절을 이끄는 역할	
whoever	anyone who (~하는 누구든지)	no matter who (누가 ~하더라도)
who(m)ever	anyone who(m) (~하는 누구든지)	no matter who(m) (누구를 ~하더라도)
whichever	anything that (~하는 것은 어느 것이든지)	no matter which (어느 것을 ~하더라도)
whatever	anything that (~하는 것은 무엇이든지)	no matter what (무엇을 ~하더라도)

예문:

- You can eat whatever you like.
- Whatever* difficulties he faces, he never gives up.
- Whichever* team you support is your choice.

* whatever과 whichever은 명사 앞에서 형용사 역할로 사용 가능

C 다음 괄호 안에서 알맞은 것을 고르시오.

1 (Who / Whoever) wants to join the club can sign up now.

2 You can eat (which / whichever) looks fresh.

3 I'll eat (whoever / whatever) you make for dinner.

복합관계부사

복합관계부사	시간, 장소 부사절	양보 부사절
	「관계부사 + ever」의 형태로 부사절을 이끄는 역할	
whenever	at any time when (~할 때는 언제나)	no matter when (언제 ~하더라도)
wherever	at any place where (~하는 곳은 어디든지)	no matter where (어디서 ~하더라도)
however	–	no matter how (아무리 ~하더라도)

예문:

- I'll call you whenever you're free.
- Wherever you look, you won't find the answer.
- However busy he is, he always makes time for his family.

D 다음 괄호 안에서 알맞은 것을 고르시오.

1 You can start (whenever / however) you're ready.

2 I'll wait for you (wherever / whichever) you are.

3 (How / However) hard you explain it, I still wouldn't understand.

A 다음 문장의 밑줄 친 부분을 한 단어로 바꿔 쓰시오.

1 She met the man, <u>and he</u> looked very familiar.　　　　→ ___________

2 I saw a group of students, <u>and they</u> were rehearsing a play.　　→ ___________

3 He bought a new phone, <u>and it</u> has a great camera.　　　→ ___________

4 He called his friends, <u>and they</u> came right away.　　　→ ___________

5 He wrote a novel, <u>and it</u> became a bestseller.　　　→ ___________

6 She read my message, <u>and it</u> surprised me.　　　→ ___________

7 I spoke to the teacher, <u>and she</u> gave me advice.　　　→ ___________

8 They canceled the event, <u>and it</u> disappointed many people.　　→ ___________

B 다음 괄호 안에서 알맞은 것을 고르시오.

1 This is the house (when / where) I grew up.

2 I don't understand the reason (why / how) she left early.

3 That was the year (when / where) we moved to the city.

4 This is the café (where / what) we had our first date.

5 She showed me (how / the way how) she folded the paper.

6 That was the moment (why / when) everyone started clapping.

7 I visited the village (when / where) my grandmother was born.

8 He didn't tell me (the way / the way how) he solved the problem.

C 다음 우리말에 맞도록 빈칸에 알맞은 말을 **보기** 에서 골라 쓰시오.

> **보기**　whoever　anyone　anything

1 먼저 끝내는 누구든지 상을 받을 것이다.

→ _________________ finishes first will get a prize.

2 나는 네가 원하는 건 어떤 것이든지 줄 것이다.

→ I'll give you _________________ that you want.

3 누가 당신을 돕든지 간에, 나는 그 사람을 신뢰할 것이다.

→ _________________ helps you, I will trust that person.

4 선반에서 네가 필요한 건 무엇이든지 가져가라.

→ Take _________________ that you need from the shelf.

5 누가 반장이 되든 나는 그 사람을 지지할 것이다.

→ I'll support _________________ who becomes the class president.

6 나는 네가 이해하지 못하는 어떤 것이든지 도와줄 것이다.

→ I will help you with _________________ that you don't understand.

D 다음 문장의 밑줄 친 부분을 한 단어로 바꿔 쓰시오.

1 네가 피곤할 때는 언제든지 쉴 수 있다.

→ You can rest <u>at any time when</u> you are tired.　　→ _________________

2 네가 안전하다고 느끼는 곳은 어디든지 더 오래 머무를 수 있다.

→ You can stay longer <u>at any place where</u> you feel safe.　→ _________________

3 그가 언제 방문하더라도, 우리는 그를 환영한다.

→ <u>No matter when</u> he visits, we welcome him.　　→ _________________

4 행사가 어디서 열리더라도, 나는 참석할 것이다.

→ <u>No matter where</u> the event is held, I'll attend.　　→ _________________

5 그가 아무리 빨리 달려도, 그는 버스를 따라잡을 수 없다.

→ <u>No matter how</u> fast he runs, he can't catch the bus.　→ _________________

A 다음 괄호 안에서 알맞은 것을 고르시오.

1   I met a student, (she / who) studies English every day.

2   She called her friend, (she / who) lives in New York.

3   They live in a big house, (it / which) has five bedrooms.

4   We called the taxi, and (it / which) arrived very quickly.

5   I saw a woman, and (she / who) looked very familiar.

6   She sent me a message, and (it / which) made me smile.

7   I know the artist, (she / who) painted this picture.

8   She bought a new laptop, (it / which) has a very fast processor.

9   We visited a castle, (which / where) was built 500 years ago.

10   They hired a new worker, (he / who) speaks four languages.

11   He apologized to me, (this / which) made me feel better.

12   They canceled the meeting, (that / which) disappointed us.

13   We visited the museum, and (it / which) was very crowded.

14   He broke his phone, (that / which) upset his parents.

15   She passed the audition, (which / where) was her dream.

16   I remember my homework, (it / which) was very important.

17   I forgot her birthday, (which / when) was really embarrassing.

18   They canceled the trip, (they / which) frustrated the students.

19   He didn't apologize, and (it / which) annoyed his friends.

20   She spoke very quietly, (this / which) made it hard to hear.

B 다음 괄호 안에서 알맞은 것을 고르시오.

1 That is the place (when / where) we celebrated her birthday.

2 I remember the time (when / where) we missed the last bus.

3 We found the place (what / where) the treasure was hidden.

4 She didn't tell me the reason (why / how) she was crying.

5 He shows me (the way / the way how) I can reset the computer.

6 I understand (what / the reason why) he left early.

7 That's (what / the place) they filmed the final scene.

8 He forgot (what / the time) the movie starts.

9 This is the café (where / which) I met my best friend.

10 Do you remember the year (why / when) we moved to Seoul?

11 He couldn't explain (the way / the way how) he solved the puzzle.

12 That was the evening (when / where) the power suddenly went out.

13 We reached a hill (when / where) we could see the entire city.

14 He told us the reason (why / how) he changed his major.

15 I love the moment (when / where) everyone starts laughing.

16 I can't forget the hour (why / when) the storm hit.

17 I know the restaurant (what / where) they serve handmade pasta.

18 We visited the island (when / where) wild horses run free.

19 That was the minute (why / when) I realized I was wrong.

20 She told me the building (why / where) the conference will be held.

C 다음 괄호 안에서 알맞은 것을 고르시오.

1   (Whom / Whoever) brings the report today can leave early.

2   Take (which / whatever) you need from here.

3   Choose (whoever / whichever) flavor you like best.

4   We'll help (who / whoever) asks for support.

5   I'll believe (whom / whatever) you say.

6   You can wear (which / whichever) matches your shoes.

7   Follow (which / whichever) path leads to the exit.

8   (What / Whatever) happens, I'll be on your side.

9   Anyone (who / whoever) studies hard can improve their grades.

10   (Whom / Whoever) helps clean the classroom will earn a reward.

11   Anyone (who / whoever) finds a lost item should take it to the office.

12   You can buy anything (who / that) you like.

13   We threw away anything (that / whichever) was old or unused.

14   I'll support you no matter (who / what) you decide.

15   No matter (who / what) knocks, don't open the door.

16   No matter (who / what) you buy, it's your choice.

17   I won't give up no matter (who / which) says I can't do it.

18   No matter (who / which) route we take, we'll arrive by noon.

19   No matter (who / which) class you choose, you'll learn a lot.

20   I'll trust you no matter (who / what) others say.

D **다음 대화의 괄호 안에서 알맞은 것을 고르시오.**

1   A: Where should I sit?

   B: Sit (whenever / wherever) you like.

2   A: When do we take a break?

   B: Take a break (whenever / whatever) you feel tired.

3   A: This homework is hard to finish.

   B: Call me (whenever / whichever) you have a question.

4   A: Do you like walking?

   B: Yes, I enjoy walking (however / wherever) there are trees and flowers.

5   A: When can I visit the library?

   B: You can go (at any time when / at any place where) it's open.

6   A: Where do you feel most relaxed?

   B: I can relax (at any time when / at any place where) I hear music.

7   A: The bus is never on time.

   B: It's delayed no matter (why / when) I go to the stop.

8   A: I think we'll be in different classrooms next year.

   B: That's fine. Let's stay friends no matter (when / where) we are.

9   A: We'll probably be on different teams.

   B: It's okay. I'll support you no matter (why / where) you play.

10   A: I don't feel confident about my speech.

   B: It'll be great no matter (how / what) nervous you feel.

A 다음 우리말에 맞도록 빈칸에 알맞은 말을 쓰시오.

1   그는 피자를 주문했는데, 그것은 끝내 도착하지 않았다.

→ He ordered pizza, ___________ never arrived.

2   나는 사촌에게서 전화를 받았는데, 그것은 나를 정말 놀라게 했다.

→ I got a call from my cousin, ___________ really surprised me.

3   그녀는 손님에게 인사했는데, 그 손님은 급해 보였다.

→ She greeted a customer, ___________ seemed to be in a hurry.

4   우리는 버스를 놓쳤는데, 그것 때문에 회의에 늦었다.

→ We missed the bus, ___________ made us late for the meeting.

5   그는 문서를 잃어버렸는데, 그 문서에는 중요한 정보가 담겨 있었다.

→ He lost a document, ___________ contained important information.

6   나는 선물을 받았는데, 그것은 금색 포장지로 아름답게 포장되어 있었다.

→ I received a gift, and ___________ was beautifully wrapped in gold paper.

7   그는 새 신발을 샀는데, 그것은 정말 멋져 보인다.

→ He bought new shoes, and ___________ look really nice.

8   우리는 이상한 소리를 들었는데, 그것은 지하실에서 들려온 것이었다.

→ We heard a strange sound, ___________ came from the basement.

9   나는 발표자들을 보았는데, 그들은 자신감 있게 말하고 있었다.

→ I saw the speakers, ___________ were speaking confidently.

10   우리는 친절한 사람들을 만났는데, 그들은 우리에게 길을 알려 주었다.

→ We met kind people, and ___________ showed us the way.

11   나는 그에게 우산을 빌려줬는데, 그것은 그를 깊이 감동시켰다.

→ I lent him an umbrella, ___________ touched him deeply.

12   우리는 문을 열어 두었는데, 그것은 고양이가 도망가게 했다.

→ We left the door open, and ___________ let the cat escape.

1 여기가 내가 가방을 두었던 장소이다.

→ This is the place ____________ I left my backpack.

2 너는 우리가 그 웃긴 사진을 찍었던 때를 기억하니?

→ Do you remember the time ____________ we took that funny photo?

3 저기는 작년에 우리가 가족 소풍을 갔던 장소이다.

→ That's the place ____________ we had our family picnic last year.

4 아무도 그가 갑자기 파티를 떠난 이유를 모른다.

→ Nobody knows the reason ____________ he suddenly left the party.

5 나는 우리가 눈 속에서 놀았던 날이 기억난다.

→ I remember the day ____________ we played in the snow.

6 여기는 우리가 항상 점심을 먹는 공원이다.

→ This is the park ____________ we always eat lunch.

7 그때는 내가 정말 행복했던 순간이었다.

→ That was the moment ____________ I felt really happy.

8 그녀가 고양이를 발견한 장소를 나에게 보여 주었다.

→ She showed me the ____________ where she found the cat.

9 나는 드디어 그녀가 운 이유를 이해했다.

→ I finally understood the reason ____________ she cried.

10 우리는 바다를 볼 수 있는 장소에 도착했다.

→ We reached a spot ____________ we could see the ocean.

11 그는 나에게 영화가 시작하는 시간을 알려 주었다.

→ He told me the ____________ when the movie starts.

12 그는 나에게 그가 문제를 푸는 방법을 보여 주었다.

→ He showed me the ____________ he solved the problem.

C 다음 우리말에 맞도록 괄호 안의 단어들을 바르게 배열하시오.

1   그는 네가 원하는 것은 무엇이든 만들 수 있다.
(can / whatever / make / you / he / want / .)

→ _______________________________________

2   너는 네가 마음에 드는 색은 어떤 것이든 고를 수 있다.
(choose / can / whichever / you / color / like / you / .)

→ _______________________________________

3   나를 웃게 하는 사람은 누구든 내 친구가 될 수 있다.
(whoever / laugh / can / makes / my friend / be / me / .)

→ _______________________________________

4   너는 네가 원하는 어떤 좌석이든 예약할 수 있다.
(you / whichever / can / you / seat / want / reserve / .)

→ _______________________________________

5   그녀는 내가 만든 것은 무엇이든 사진을 찍었다.
(I / whatever / made / took / she / a picture of / .)

→ _______________________________________

6   질문이 있는 사람은 누구든 손을 들어야 한다.
(anyone / raise / must / has / who / a question / their hand / .)

→ _______________________________________

7   나는 네가 추천하는 것은 무엇이든 읽을 것이다.
(recommend / anything / will / I / you / that / read / .)

→ _______________________________________

8   나는 그가 고장낸 것은 무엇이든지 고쳤다.
(fixed / that / broke / I / anything / he / .)

→ _______________________________________

9   네가 어느 버스를 타더라도, 너는 시청에 갈 수 있다.
(you / get to / can / bus / the city hall / no matter which / take, / you / .)

→ _______________________________________

10   네가 무엇을 선택하더라도, 너의 가족이 지지해 줄 것이다.
(no matter what / choose, / will / you / your family / you / support / .)

→ _______________________________________

D 다음 우리말에 맞도록 괄호 안의 단어들을 바르게 배열하시오.

1 너는 네가 원할 때는 언제든지 나에게 전화할 수 있다.
(call / whenever / you / me / can / want / you / .)

→ ____

2 그들은 가는 곳마다 어디서든 친구를 사귄다.
(make / they / friends / wherever / go / they / .)

→ ____

3 우리는 그를 볼 때마다 그에게 인사했다.
(him / we / whenever / greeted / saw / we / him /.)

→ ____

4 네가 어디에 있든지 너는 영어를 공부할 수 있다.
(English / study / wherever / you / can / are / you / .)

→ ____

5 그는 배가 고플 때는 언제나 간식을 먹는다.
(a snack / at any time when / hungry / he / is / eats / he / .)

→ ____

6 그가 노래하는 곳은 어디든지 사람들이 모인다.
(sings / he / gather / people / at any place where / .)

→ ____

7 네가 그것을 어떻게 해석하든, 결과는 같다.
(is / however / interpret / the result / the same / you / it, / .)

→ ____

8 우리가 언제 떠나더라도, 도착 시간은 같다.
(leave, / we / the arrival time / the same / is / no matter when / .)

→ ____

9 네가 어디에 있더라도, 나는 너를 찾을 것이다.
(find / will / no matter where / you / I / are, / you / .)

→ ____

10 내가 아무리 설명하더라도, 그는 그것을 이해할 수 없다.
(no matter how / understand / he / explain, / I / can't / that / .)

→ ____

1 다음 중 밑줄 친 부분이 어법상 <u>틀린</u> 것을 모두 고르시오.

① I met Sam, <u>who</u> is my neighbor.

② She opened a box, <u>which</u> had a gift inside.

③ We saw Ben, <u>whom</u> plays soccer.

④ She picked a flower, <u>that</u> smelled nice.

⑤ I read a story, <u>which</u> made me laugh.

[2-3] 다음 중 빈칸에 들어갈 말로 가장 적절한 것을 고르시오.

2

> That's the day _________ I got the highest score on the test.

① who　　② which

③ when　　④ where

⑤ why

3

> This is the house _________ I lived when I was a child.

① when　　② where

③ why　　④ how

⑤ what

4 다음 중 밑줄 친 부분이 어법상 <u>틀린</u> 것은?

① I remember the time <u>when</u> I made a big mistake.

② That's the place <u>where</u> I took the picture.

③ This is the reason <u>why</u> I was late.

④ He talked about the time <u>when</u> he first stood on stage.

⑤ This is the classroom <u>why</u> I first learned English.

[5-6] 다음 중 어법상 <u>틀린</u> 것을 고르시오.

5

① That was the time when the rain stopped.

② This is the place where I learned to ride a bike.

③ I want to know the reason why you are smiling.

④ I don't like the way how he talks to others.

⑤ I know the reason she is upset.

6

① I'll help whoever needs my support.

② Whichever you decide is okay with me.

③ I'll eat anything which you cook.

④ Anyone who studies every day will succeed.

⑤ Whatever he said was true.

보기 whoever   whichever   anyone

7

네가 어느 것을 선택하든 괜찮다.

→ ______________ you choose will be fine.

8

먼저 도착하는 사람은 누구든 불을 켜야 한다.

→ ______________ arrives first should turn on the lights.

9

열심히 공부하는 사람은 누구든 자신의 목표를 이룰 것이다

→ ______________ who studies hard will achieve his or her goal.

[10-11] 다음 문장에서 어법상 **틀린** 곳을 찾아 바르게 고치시오.

10

No matter why tries to stop me, I won't give up.

______________ → ______________

11

Anything who wants more information can ask the teacher.

______________ → ______________

12 다음 글의 밑줄 친 부분 중 어법상 **틀린** 곳은?

Tom went to the park on Saturday. He played soccer with ①whoever wanted to join. After the game, he shared snacks and said, "You can have ②whatever you like." He didn't care no matter ③who sat next to him on the bench. No matter ④who drink his friends chose, he was happy. He gave anything ⑤that he had to make everyone smile.

①   ②   ③   ④   ⑤

[13-14] 다음 대화의 빈칸에 들어갈 말로 가장 적절한 것을 고르시오.

13

A: This homework is really difficult for me.
B: Don't give up, ___________ hard it is.

① what
② whom
③ whoever
④ whichever
⑤ however

14

A: I'll wait for your message.
B: Okay, I'll text you ___________ I have time.

① whatever
② wherever
③ however
④ whenever
⑤ whoever

[15-17] 다음 우리말에 맞도록 빈칸에 알맞은 한 단어를 쓰시오.

15

네가 준비되었을 때 언제든지 게임을 시작해도 된다.

→ You can start the game at any time ___________ you're ready.

16

그는 조용하고 어두운 곳이라면 어디에서든 잘 수 있다.

→ He can sleep ___________ it's quiet and dark.

17

상황이 아무리 스트레스 받을 정도로 힘들어도, 그녀는 침착함을 유지한다.

→ ___________ stressful the situation is, she stays calm.

18 다음 중 밑줄 친 부분이 어법상 틀린 것은?

① I'll go <u>wherever</u> you want to go.
② You can wear <u>whatever</u> you like.
③ <u>Whoever</u> arrives first gets a gift.
④ <u>However</u> hard you explain, I still don't get it.
⑤ We can meet <u>whichever</u> you're free.

19

나는 그가 회의에 참석하지 않은 이유를 알고 있다.
(the meeting / why / I / the reason / he /
know / didn't attend / .)

→ _______________________________________

20

네가 무슨 생각을 하든지, 그것은 네 선택이다.
(it's / no / your / what / you / matter /
think, / choice / .)

→ _______________________________________

[21–22] 다음 두 대화의 빈칸에 들어갈 말이 바르게
짝지어진 것을 고르시오.

21

- A: Do you know the place __________
  I can charge my phone?
  B: There's a café around the corner.
- A: Tell me the reason __________ you
  were absent yesterday.
  B: I wasn't feeling well.

① what - which

② where - why

③ where - what

④ when - whichever

⑤ that - whoever

22

- A: You can sit __________ seat you want.
  B: I'll take the one by the window.
- A: I do my homework carefully, but
  I still make mistakes.
  B: Yeah, mistakes happen __________
  hard you try.

① whichever - whenever

② whichever - however

③ whatever - wherever

④ wherever - whenever

⑤ however - whichever

23 다음 글의 밑줄 친 부분 중 어법상 옳은 것끼리 바르게 짝지어진 것은?

Semi is a kind student.
ⓐWhenever someone needs
help, she is always ready to help.
ⓑWherever she goes, she makes
people feel happy. ⓒHow long
people's stories are, she listens
patiently. No matter ⓓthat
happens, she stays calm and kind.
And no matter ⓔhowever hard
things get, she never gives up.

① ⓐ, ⓑ

② ⓑ, ⓒ

③ ⓑ, ⓓ

④ ⓐ, ⓑ, ⓔ

⑤ ⓑ, ⓓ, ⓔ

분사

- 분사
- 감정을 나타내는 분사
- 분사구문 만들기
- 분사구문의 다양한 의미

분사

	동사를 변형시켜 형용사처럼 쓰는 단어 (명사 수식 또는 보어 자리)	
	현재분사	과거분사
형태	동사 + -ing	동사 + -ed(또는 불규칙 변화형)
의미	진행 중인 동작, 능동: ~하고 있는, ~하는	완료된 상태, 수동: ~한, ~된
예시	a sleeping baby (잠자는 아기) a broken toy (망가진 장난감) I saw a bird flying in the sky. (나는 새가 날고 있는 것을 보았다.)	

A 다음 그림에 맞도록 괄호 안에서 알맞은 것을 고르시오.

1 a (cried / crying) child

2 a (broken / breaking) doll

3 a girl (read / reading) a book

4 the cookies (baked / baking) this morning

감정을 나타내는 분사

원형	현재분사	과거분사	원형	현재분사	과거분사
annoy (짜증나게 하다)	annoying (짜증나게 하는)	annoyed (짜증난)	depress (우울하게 하다)	depressing (우울하게 하는)	depressed (우울한)
interest (흥미를 갖게 하다)	interesting (흥미로운)	interested (흥미를 느끼는)	surprise (놀라게 하다)	surprising (놀라게 하는)	surprised (놀란)
excite (흥분시키다)	exciting (신나게 하는)	excited (신이 난)	disgust (역겹게 만들다)	disgusting (역겹게 하는)	disgusted (역겨운)
bore (지루하게 하다)	boring (지루하게 하는)	bored (지루한)	frighten (겁나게 하다)	frightening (겁먹게 하는)	frightened (겁먹은)

현재분사(-ing): 주어가 감정을 일으키는 대상 → The lecture is boring.
과거분사(-ed): 주어가 감정을 느끼는 사람 → I am bored during the lecture.

B 괄호 안에 주어진 단어 중 알맞은 것을 고르시오.

1 This noise is (annoyed / annoying).

2 I'm so (excited / exciting) for the trip!

3 This book is really (interested / interesting).

분사구문: 부사절의 접속사와 주어를 없애고, 분사로 시작하는 간단한 형태로 바꾼 것

❶ 부사절의 접속사 생략 *의미를 분명히 하기 위해 접속사를 생략하지 않기도 함
❷ 부사절의 주어가 주절의 주어와 같으면 생략(같지 않으면 남겨둠)
❸ 부사절의 시제가 주절의 시제와 같으면 동사를 분사(~ing)로(부정: Not + ing),
　주절의 시제보다 하나 앞선 시제이면 「having + 과거분사」로 바꿈 *Being, having been은 생략 가능

예시

주어 같음: 생략
Because he felt hungry, he ate a sandwich.
❸ 시제 같음: +ing
→　　　　Feeling hungry, he ate a sandwich.

C 다음 문장을 분사구문으로 만들 때 빈칸에 알맞은 <u>한 단어</u>를 쓰시오.

Because he was born in Italy, he could speak Italian fluently.

→ ______________ in Italy, he could speak Italian fluently.

분사구문의 다양한 의미

의미	예문
이유 (as, because, since)	Because I was tired, I took a nap. → Being tired, I took a nap. (피곤했기 때문에, 나는 낮잠을 잤다.)
시간, 때 (as, when, while, after)	When he heard the bell, he left the room. → Hearing the bell, he left the room. (종소리를 듣고, 그는 방을 나갔다.)
양보 (though, although)	Though she tried her best, she didn't win the contest. → Trying her best, she didn't win the contest. (최선을 다했음에도, 그녀는 대회에서 우승하지 못했다.)
조건 (if)	If you finish your homework, you can play outside. → Finishing your homework, you can play outside. (숙제를 끝내면, 너는 밖에서 놀 수 있다.)
동시동작 (as, while)	While she walked in the park, she listened to music. → Walking in the park, she listened to music. (공원을 걸으며, 그녀는 음악을 들었다.)

D 괄호 안의 단어를 이용하여 빈칸에 알맞은 말을 쓰시오.

1　Being hungry, I ate a sandwich. (because)

→ ______________ ______________ ______________ hungry, I ate a sandwich.

2　Arriving, they found us eating. (when)

→ ______________ ______________ arrived, they found us eating.

A 다음 문장에서 밑줄 친 부분이 분사로 쓰였으면 ○, 아니면 X를 표시하시오.

1 I see a <u>sleeping</u> dog.　　　　　　(　)

2 I enjoy <u>reading</u> books.　　　　　　(　)

3 He found a <u>smiling</u> girl.　　　　　(　)

4 We found a <u>singing</u> bird.　　　　　(　)

5 She watched a <u>crying</u> baby.　　　　(　)

6 They noticed a <u>running</u> boy.　　　　(　)

7 <u>Running</u> is good for your health.　　(　)

8 She likes <u>swimming</u> in the morning.　(　)

B 다음 괄호 안에서 알맞은 것을 고르시오.

1 They saw a (buzz / buzzing) bee.

2 Mom washed a (stained / staining) shirt.

3 He got (bored / boring) after ten minutes.

4 My father fixed the (broke / broken) clock.

5 He pointed at a (painted / painting) vase.

6 He saw Jim (ran / running) in the classroom.

7 Mr. Hong found a (yawned / yawning) student.

8 The game became (bored / boring) after a while.

C 예시 를 참고하여 빈칸에 알맞은 <u>한 단어</u>를 쓰시오.

> 예시   Because he felt tired, he took a rest.
> → <u>Feeling</u> tired, he took a rest.

1 When she smiled, she made me feel better.

→ _________________, she made me feel better.

2 While she was reading a book, she heard a loud noise.

→ _________________ a book, she heard a loud noise.

3 Though she is young, she's very smart.

→ _________________ young, she's very smart.

4 As I had no money, I didn't buy the book.

→ _________________ no money, I didn't buy the book.

5 Because it was cold, I wore a coat.

→ _________________ _________________ cold, I wore a coat.

D 다음 빈칸에 알맞은 말을 써서 부사절 문장을 완성하시오.

1 Finishing early, I'll help you.

→ If _________________________ early, I'll help you.

2 It being rainy, we played outside.

→ Though _________________________, we played outside.

3 The lights going out, we lit a candle.

→ When _________________________ out, we lit a candle.

4 The bell ringing, the students became quiet.

→ As _________________________, the students became quiet.

5 While cleaning my room, I found a coin.

→ While _________________________ my room, I found a coin.

A 다음 중 밑줄 친 부분이 현재분사이면 ○, 과거분사이면 △, 동명사이면 X를 표시하시오.

1 He saw the <u>torn</u> flag. ( )

2 Look at the <u>rolling</u> ball. ( )

3 Orion is a set of <u>shining</u> stars. ( )

4 He grabbed a <u>frozen</u> banana. ( )

5 We watched a <u>swimming</u> baby. ( )

6 <u>Reading</u> in bed helps me relax. ( )

7 He interviewed a <u>running</u> child. ( )

8 I enjoy <u>listening</u> to K-pop music. ( )

9 The dog followed a <u>climbing</u> cat. ( )

10 Mom smiled at the <u>crawling</u> baby. ( )

11 She avoided <u>answering</u> the question. ( )

12 The girl pointed at a <u>shaking</u> tree. ( )

13 He saw a car being <u>washed</u> near the fence. ( )

14 <u>Swimming</u> in the river is dangerous. ( )

15 They threw away the <u>spoiled</u> sandwich. ( )

16 <u>Watching</u> TV late at night is not good for your health. ( )

17 They are interested in <u>learning</u> English. ( )

18 The baby was scared of the <u>barking</u> dog. ( )

19 Ms. Kang found the watch <u>lost</u> at the park. ( )

20 A rabbit found a turtle <u>sleeping</u> under the tree. ( )

1   I like the bird (sang / singing) in the morning.

2   He drew a blue bird (flies / flying) in the sky.

3   They opened a box (sealed / sealing) with tape.

4   I noticed a straw (bent / bending) near a cup.

5   The girl found a puppy (played / playing) alone.

6   A cat followed a ball (rolled / rolling) on the mat.

7   I kicked a ball (stuck / sticking) under the bench.

8   She reached for a hat (blown / blowing) by the wind.

9   We witnessed a balloon (rose / rising) above the rooftop.

10   She encountered a squirrel (runs / running) up a tree.

11   That girl spotted a cat (rested / resting) on the bed.

12   The boy grabbed a dog (barked / barking) in the bush.

13   She passed a note (folded / folding) into a small square.

14   He stopped at a path (blocked / blocking) by fallen rocks.

15   There is a kitten (meowed / meowing) outside the window.

16   The dog smelled a flower (crushed / crushing) by someone.

17   The child held an egg (cracked / cracking) in the kitchen.

18   The boy (laughed / laughing) near the gate is my brother.

19   A woman was looking at her son (jumped / jumping) at the park.

20   The boy touched a statue (damaged / damaging) by the storm.

C 다음 대화의 괄호 안에서 알맞은 것을 고르시오.

1 A: Is she (interested / interesting) in art?

    B: Yes, she has always been (interested / interesting) in painting.

2 A: Did she look (bored / boring) in class?

    B: Yes, the lecture was really (bored / boring) today.

3 A: Were they (annoyed / annoying) by the delay?

    B: Yes, the (annoyed / annoying) passengers waited for hours.

4 A: I felt (frightened / frightening) in the dark.

    B: Me, too. The sound was really (frightened / frightening).

5 A: Wasn't that an (interested / interesting) idea?

    B: Yes, everyone looked (interested / interesting) in it.

6 A: Did you help paint the wall (scratched / scratching) by the cat?

    B: Yes, and we cleaned off the dirt (sticking / stuck) to it.

7 A: It was an (excited / exciting) day at the park.

    B: Right. The (excited / exciting) kids played all afternoon.

8 A: Were you (depressed / depressing) by the news today?

    B: Yes, it was such a (depressed / depressing) report.

9 A: The ending was really (surprised / surprising).

    B: You're right. The audience looked really (surprised / surprising).

10 A: Were you (disgusted / disgusting) by the smell in the kitchen?

    B: Yes, the (disgusted / disgusting) garbage hadn't been taken out for days.

 다음 두 문장의 의미가 같도록 빈칸에 알맞은 말을 쓰시오. (단, 분사구문 문장을 만들 것)

1 If she works hard, she'll succeed.

= ___________________ ___________________, she'll succeed.

2 Though I was tired, I kept working.

= ___________________ ___________________, I kept working.

3 If we hurry, we can catch the bus.

= ___________________, we can catch the bus.

4 Since he was sick, he stayed home.

= ___________________ ___________________, he stayed home.

5 Since I lost my keys, I can't get in.

= ___________________ ___________________ my keys, I can't get in.

6 As she was exhausted, she went to bed early.

= ___________________ ___________________, she went to bed early.

7 When I opened the window, I saw a bird fly in.

= ___________________ the window, I saw a bird fly in.

8 While he was cooking, he cleaned the room.

= While ___________________, he cleaned the room.

9 Because he liked her, he bought her some flowers.

= ___________________ her, he bought her some flowers.

10 While I was jogging in the morning, I listened to music.

= ___________________ in the morning, I listened to music.

11 Because she didn't study, she failed the test.

= ___________________ ___________________, she failed the test.

12 As it was getting dark, we decided to go home.

= ___________________ ___________________ dark, we decided to go home.

A 다음 우리말에 맞도록 괄호 안의 단어를 이용하여 빈칸에 알맞은 말을 쓰시오.

1 나는 연을 날리고 있는 아이를 보았다. (fly)

→ I saw a child ________________ a kite.

2 한 여자가 도로에 누워 있는 고양이를 보았다. (lie)

→ A woman saw a cat ________________ on the road.

3 그녀는 큰 공을 굴리고 있는 딸을 발견했다. (roll)

→ She spotted her daughter ________________ a big ball.

4 너는 소파에서 기지개를 켜고 있는 고양이가 보이니? (stretch)

→ Can you see the cat ________________ on the sofa?

5 내 동생은 강아지에게 찢긴 종이 조각을 모았다. (tear)

→ My brother collected the pieces of paper ________________ by the dog.

6 그 관리인은 바람에 깨진 창문을 치웠다. (break)

→ The janitor removed the window ________________ by wind.

7 과학자는 실험실에서 돌아가는 바퀴를 관찰했다. (turn)

→ A scientist observed a wheel ________________ in the lab.

8 아이는 호수로 뛰어드는 새를 보았다. (dive)

→ A child saw a bird ________________ into the lake.

9 그는 길 건너편에서 손을 흔드는 친구를 알아보았다. (wave)

→ He recognized his friend ________________ across the street.

10 한 아이가 비행기 모양으로 접혀 있는 종이를 주웠다. (fold)

→ A child picked up a paper ________________ into a plane.

11 새끼 고양이가 물어뜯어 망가진 공을 가지고 놀고 있었다. (damage)

→ A kitten was playing with a ball ________________ from chewing.

12 이웃은 공원에서 그네를 타고 있는 소녀를 발견했다. (swing)

→ The neighbor found a girl ________________ in the park.

 다음 우리말에 맞도록 괄호 안의 단어를 이용하여 빈칸에 알맞은 말을 쓰시오.

1 그들은 하얗게 칠해진 문을 알아차리지 못했다. (paint)

→ They didn't notice the door ___________________ white.

2 그들은 회의를 하는 동안 우울해 보였다. (depress)

→ They looked ___________________ during the meeting.

3 내 친구는 바닥에 놓여 있는 수건을 나에게 건넸다. (lie)

→ My friend handed me the towel ___________________ on the floor.

4 그들은 나무 옆에 닫혀 있는 창문 하나를 발견했다. (close)

→ They found a window ___________________ beside the tree.

5 요리를 하고 있을 때, 나는 전화벨이 울리는 것을 들었다. (cook)

→ ___________________, I heard the phone ring.

6 기차를 기다리는 동안에, 나는 책을 읽었다. (wait)

→ While ___________________ for the train, I read a book.

7 교통 체증에 갇혀서, 나는 회의에 늦었다. (trap)

→ ___________________ in traffic, I arrived late to the meeting.

8 결과에 만족해서, 그는 자랑스럽게 미소 지었다. (satisfy)

→ ___________________ with the result, he smiled proudly.

9 일에 지쳐서, 그는 바로 잠자리에 들었다. (exhaust)

→ ___________________ from work, he went straight to bed.

10 그 소식에 놀라서, 그녀는 휴대폰을 떨어뜨렸다. (surprise)

→ ___________________ by the news, she dropped her phone.

11 기쁨에 차서, 그녀는 주위 사람들을 모두 껴안았다. (fill)

→ ___________________ with joy, she hugged everyone around her.

12 저녁 식사를 하고 나서, 우리는 산책을 갔다. (eat)

→ After ___________________ dinner, we went for a walk.

C 다음 우리말에 맞도록 괄호 안의 단어들을 바르게 배열하시오.

1 그 윙윙거리는 소리는 정말 성가시다.
(sound / that buzzing / annoying / so / is / .)

→ ____

2 우리는 속삭이는 남자아이를 보았다.
(boy / saw / we / whispering / a / .)

→ ____

3 우리는 타 버린 냄비를 씻었다.
(the / we / washed / pan / burned / .)

→ ____

4 너는 깜박이는 불빛을 보았다.
(watched / you / blinking / light / the / .)

→ ____

5 강아지는 기어다니는 벌레를 따라갔다.
(bug / followed / the puppy / a / creeping / .)

→ ____

6 그 소년은 파란색 글씨로 쓴 편지를 보냈다.
(in blue / the boy / a letter / written / sent / .)

→ ____

7 그녀는 울타리로 인해 찢어진 셔츠를 수선했다.
(the shirt / she / the fence / by / torn / sewed up / .)

→ ____

8 그들은 손상된 창문을 고쳤다.
(window / they / damaged / the / fixed / .)

→ ____

9 그들은 경기 전에 신이 났다.
(excited / they / the game / felt / before / .)

→ ____

10 그는 벽에 붙어 있는 포스터를 발견했다.
(he / a poster / found / the wall / to / attached / .)

→ ____

 다음 중 분사구문은 부사절로, 부사절은 분사구문으로 바꿔 다시 쓰시오.
(단, 괄호 안에 단어가 있는 경우 알맞게 이용할 것)

1 Because I loved music, I joined the band.

→ ____

2 While we were walking, we saw a rainbow.

→ ____

3 As he was not ready, he made us wait.

→ ____

4 Since we finished, we can relax now.

→ ____

5 Because he had forgotten his umbrella, he got wet.

→ ____

6 As the weather was bad, we stayed indoors.

→ ____

7 Turning around the corner, I saw a cat. (when)

→ ____

8 Studying, you will pass the exam. (if)

→ ____

9 The movie ending, everyone clapped. (when)

→ ____

10 Caught in the rain, they ran into a shop. (because)

→ ____

11 Ruined by the fire, the building was rebuilt later. (because)

→ ____

12 Built in 1887, the tower is a famous landmark. (because)

→ ____

혼공실전 3

1

> I bought a _______ book.

① use   ② uses

③ used   ④ using

⑤ to use

2

> She caught a boy _______ on the desk.

① jump   ② jumps

③ jumped   ④ jumping

⑤ to jump

3 다음 밑줄 친 부분과 쓰임이 다른 것을 <u>모두</u> 고르시오.

> The <u>barking</u> dog was very loud.

① He enjoys <u>dancing</u>.

② The <u>crying</u> baby fell asleep.

③ <u>Swimming</u> is my favorite sport.

④ I heard a dog <u>barking</u> last night.

⑤ She saw a cat <u>climbing</u> the tree.

4

① That was an excited game!

② He moved the broken chair.

③ We replaced the melt ice cream.

④ I'm interesting in learning French.

⑤ It's annoyed when people talk during movies.

5

① They fixed a printer jamming in the office.

② He read a handwrite letter from his friend.

③ They saw a cave hide under the rocks.

④ A girl saw a note written by her friend.

⑤ The boy found a curtain tearing at the window.

6

> That was a ___________ result.

① surprise

② surprises

③ surprised

④ surprising

⑤ to surprise

7

He looked _________ when he saw the dog.

① frighten
② frightens
③ frightened
④ frightening
⑤ to frighten

[8-9] 다음 우리말에 맞도록 빈칸에 알맞은 말을 쓰시오.

8

수학은 때때로 지루할 수 있다.

→ Math can be _____________ sometimes.

9

그는 이별 후에 우울함을 느꼈다.

→ He felt _____________ after the breakup.

[10-11] 다음 두 문장의 의미가 같도록 빈칸에 알맞은 말을 쓰시오.

10

As I was walking, I saw an old friend.

= _______________, I saw an old friend.

11

Since the light is red, we must stop.

= _______________ _______________

_______________ red, we must stop.

12 다음 중 어법상 틀린 것을 고르시오.

① The man opened a closed door.
② She showed me the torn page.
③ He walked past a cracked mirror.
④ Crying, she got a tissue from me.
⑤ Starting to rain, we ran inside.

13 다음 중 어법상 <u>틀린</u> 문장을 모두 고르면?

① Though trying hard, they failed.

② While playing, it started to snow.

③ Having apologized, he was forgiven.

④ Wear black, she looked elegant.

⑤ Shocked by the result, I couldn't say a word.

[14-15] 다음 대화의 빈칸에 들어갈 말이 바르게 짝지어진 것을 고르시오.

14

A: Don't step on the _________ tile.
B: Oh, thanks! _________ it, I almost stepped on it.

① breaking – Not noticing

② breaking – Not noticed

③ broken – Not noticing

④ broken – Not noticed

⑤ broken – Noticing not

15

A: _________ by the trip, my children couldn't sleep at all last night.
B: _________ for our vacation, my son smiled all day.

① Exciting – Waiting

② Excited – Waiting

③ Exciting – Waited

④ Excited – Waited

⑤ Excite – Wait

[16-17] 다음 문장에서 어법상 <u>틀린</u> 곳을 찾아 바르게 고치시오.

16

My sister was shocking because she found a big spider in the closet.

_________________ → _________________

17

Knowing for his honesty, he was trusted by everyone.

_________________ → _________________

[18-19] 다음 우리말에 맞도록 괄호 안의 단어들을 바르게 배열하시오.

18

기타를 치고 있는 소년은 내 남동생이다.
(the guitar / the boy / is / playing / my brother / .)

→ _________________

19

그 대회를 위해 선택된 책은 매우 두꺼웠다.
(chosen / the book / for the contest /
very thick / was / .)

→ ______________________________________

22 다음 대화에서 어법상 틀린 곳을 찾아 바르게 고치시오.

A: The movie was really frightened,
   wasn't it?
B: Yes, I was so scared during the
   scene with the haunted house!

______________ → ______________

[20-21] 다음 우리말에 맞도록 밑줄 친 부분을 접속사가 있는 문장으로 바꾸어 쓰시오.

20

선생님이 들어오셨을 때, 학생들은 일어섰다.
→ The teacher entering, the students
   stood up.

→ ______________________________________

23 다음 글의 밑줄 친 부분 중 어법상 옳은 것끼리 바르게 짝지어진 것은?

ⓐEnjoying the cool autumn
breeze, Sandra sat on a bench
near the pond. Suddenly, a gentle
wind blew, and she watched the
leaves ⓑfallen from the tree. A
woman passed by, carrying a small
child in her arms. ⓒSurrounded by
nature, Sandra felt ⓓrelaxing. She
took out her notebook. ⓔInspired
by the peaceful scene, she began
to write a poem about the beauty
of fall.

① ⓐ, ⓓ
② ⓑ, ⓓ
③ ⓐ, ⓑ, ⓒ
④ ⓐ, ⓒ, ⓔ
⑤ ⓑ, ⓒ, ⓓ

21

그는 방에 혼자 남겨졌기 때문에, 울기 시작했다.
→ Left alone in the room, he started
   crying.

→ ______________________________________

4

과거완료와 가정법

- 과거완료의 형태와 개념
- 가정법 현재와 가정법 과거
- 가정법 과거완료
- I wish / as if 가정법

과거완료의 형태와 개념

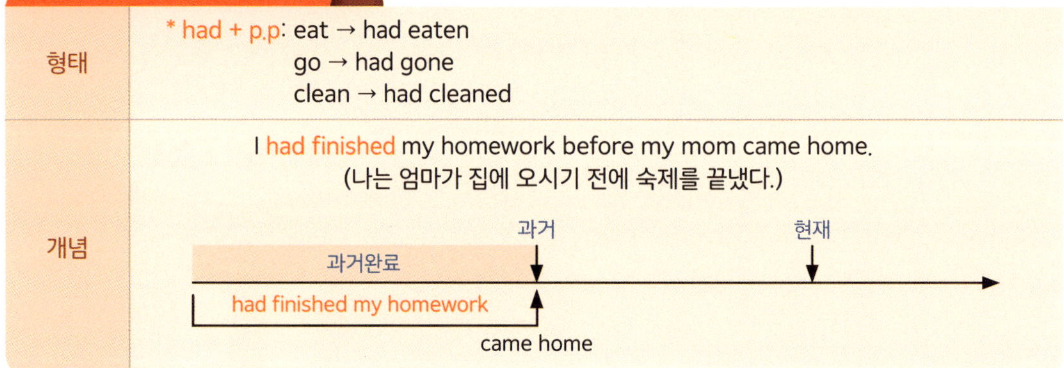

형태	* had + p.p: eat → had eaten go → had gone clean → had cleaned
개념	I had finished my homework before my mom came home. (나는 엄마가 집에 오시기 전에 숙제를 끝냈다.)

A 다음 괄호 안에서 알맞은 것을 고르시오.

1 He was excited because he (has fixed / had fixed) his car.

2 (Did / Had) Jake closed the door before the music started?

3 Tom (hadn't / hasn't) wrapped the package when I came back.

가정법 현재와 가정법 과거

	설명	형태 / 예문
가정법 현재 (조건문)	현실적으로 일어날 가능성이 있는 일을 가정	If + 주어 + 현재형 동사, 주어 + [will / may / can] + 동사원형 • If it is sunny, we will go hiking. (만약 날씨가 맑다면, 우리는 하이킹을 갈 것이다.)
가정법 과거	현재 사실과 반대되거나 일어날 가능성이 희박한 상황을 가정	If + 주어 + 과거형 동사 / were, 주어 + [would / could / might] + 동사원형 • If I were you, I would take the job. (내가 너라면, 그 일을 맡을 텐데.) • If he knew the answer, he would tell me. (그가 정답을 안다면, 나에게 말해줄 텐데.)

B 다음 두 문장의 의미가 같도록 괄호 안의 단어를 이용하여 빈칸에 알맞은 단어를 쓰시오.
(단, 필요시 어형을 바꿀 것)

1 She has the ability to pass the test. She just needs to study.

= If she ______________, she ______________ pass the test. (study, will)

2 It's rainy now, so we can't go hiking.

= If it ______________ sunny now, we ______________ go hiking. (be, can)

과거 사실과 반대되는 상황을 가정, 이미 지나간 일에 대한 아쉬움이나 후회를 표현

형태: If + 주어 + had p.p, 주어 + [would / could / might] + have p.p

예문:
- If I had studied hard, I would have passed the exam.
  (내가 열심히 공부했더라면, 시험에 합격했을 텐데.)
- If I had been a bird, I would have flown to you.
  (내가 새였더라면, 당신에게 날아갔을 텐데.)

C 다음 문장을 우리말로 해석하시오.

1 If she had left earlier, she would have caught the bus.

  → ____

2 If I had been strong, I could have carried the box.

  → ____

I wish / as if 가정법

가정법	형태 / 설명 / 의미	예문
I wish	주어 + 과거형 동사 / were 현재 이루지 못한 소망을 가정 (~라면 좋을 텐데)	I wish I were taller. (내가 키가 더 크면 좋을 텐데.)
	주어 + had + 과거분사 과거에 이루지 못한 소망을 가정 (~였다면 좋을 텐데)	I wish I had studied hard. (내가 열심히 공부했었더라면 좋을 텐데.)
as if	주어 + 과거형 동사 / were 현재 사실과 반대되는 상황을 가정 (마치 ~인 것처럼)	He acts as if he knew everything. (그는 마치 모든 것을 알고 있는 것처럼 행동한다.)
	주어 + had + 과거분사 과거 사실과 반대되는 상황을 가정 (마치 ~였던 것처럼)	She talks as if she had seen a ghost. (그녀는 마치 유령을 보았던 것처럼 말한다.)

D 다음 두 문장의 의미가 같도록 괄호 안에서 알맞은 것을 고르시오.

1 I don't think I can pass the exam, but I want to.

   = I wish I (can pass / could pass) the exam.

2 In fact, she is not my mother.

   = She scolds me as if she (is / were) my mother.

A 다음 괄호 안에서 알맞은 것을 고르시오.

1 He was full because he (has eaten / had eaten) a big lunch.

2 I (feed / had fed) the cat, so it lay down and slept.

3 Jake (has bought / had bought) the TV before the vacation ended.

4 The girl that (draws / had drawn) the picture showed it proudly.

5 We (hadn't written / had written) the report, so we presented it in class.

6 Emily (has finished / had finished) the project before the meeting started.

7 The boy who (studies / had studied) all night fell asleep during class.

8 He (arrived / had arrived) at the station before the train left.

B 다음 괄호 안에서 알맞은 것을 고르시오.

1 If she asks questions, she (will / would) learn more.

2 If he (uses / used) sunscreen, he will avoid sunburn.

3 If they (call / would call) her, they will get the answer.

4 If she takes notes, she (remembered / will remember) the material.

5 If we walked to school, it (takes / would take) a long time.

6 He (learned / would learn) more if he read books.

7 If he (helps / helped) his mom, she could finish it soon.

8 He might buy a new phone if he (saved / will save) money.

C 다음 우리말에 맞도록 괄호 안의 단어를 이용하여 가정법 과거완료 문장을 완성하시오.

1 내가 거기에 있었더라면, 나는 그것을 했을 텐데. (be)

→ If I _________________ there, I would have done it.

2 내가 돈이 많이 있었더라면, 나는 그 차를 살 수 있었을 텐데. (have)

→ If I _________________ much money, I could have bought the car.

3 그가 제때 그것을 끝냈더라면, 우리는 늦지 않았을 텐데. (finish)

→ If he _________________ it in time, we wouldn't have been late.

4 그녀가 내 충고를 받아들였더라면, 그녀는 행복했을 텐데. (take)

→ If she _________________ my advice, she would have been happy.

5 눈이 오지 않았다면, 우리는 산에 오를 수 있었을 텐데. (snow)

→ If it _________________, we could have climbed the mountain.

D 다음 두 문장의 의미가 같도록 빈칸에 알맞은 단어를 쓰시오.

1 I don't live in Jeju, but I want to.

= I wish I _____________ in Jeju.

2 I didn't pass the exam, and I feel sorry about it now.

= I wish I _____________ _____________ the exam.

3 I didn't take notes, and I regret it now.

= I wish I _____________ _____________ notes.

4 In fact, he is not rich.

= He acts as if he _____________ rich.

5 In fact, he didn't win the prize, but he acts like he did.

= He acts as if he _____________ _____________ the prize.

A 다음 괄호 안에서 알맞은 것을 고르시오.

1 (Had / Did) Tom left the room already?

2 The bus (has not arrived / had not arrived) until now.

3 He (has never eaten / had never eaten) raw fish so far.

4 Junho (studies / had studied) before he took the test.

5 They (have lived / had lived) in Seoul since they were young.

6 I (knew / have known) her since elementary school.

7 I (study / had studied) the map, so I didn't get lost.

8 We (packed / had packed) everything before the taxi arrived.

9 (Has / Had) she printed the report before it went missing?

10 (Has / Had) she already seen the movie before you bought the tickets?

11 She (has lost / had lost) her phone, so she borrowed mine.

12 (Has / Had) he repaired the bike before he rode it to school?

13 She (reads / had read) the letter just before the class began.

14 They (open / had opened) the gift just before the party started.

15 He (has finished / had finished) his homework, so he watched TV.

16 Her sister (draws / had drawn) the picture before the lights went out.

17 They (had cleaned / have cleaned) the room, so their mom was happy.

18 Tom (has done / had done) the homework when I opened the door.

19 The chef who (has cooked / had cooked) the meal greeted the guests.

20 She (lived / had lived) in the countryside before she moved here.

B **다음 우리말에 맞도록 괄호 안에서 알맞은 것을 고르시오.**

1 네가 안전벨트를 매지 않으면, 벌금을 물게 될 것이다.

→ If you (don't / didn't) wear the seatbelt, you will get a fine.

2 네가 돈을 모으면, 새 이어폰을 살 수 있을 것이다.

→ If you (save / saved) money, you will be able to buy new earbuds.

3 내 남동생이 연습을 하면, 게임에서 이길 것이다.

→ If my brother (practices / practiced), he will win the game.

4 그들이 일찍 일어나면, 제시간에 도착할 것이다.

→ If they (wake / woke) up early, they will arrive on time.

5 네가 수업에 집중하면, 많은 것을 배울 것이다.

→ If you focus in class, you (will / would) learn a lot.

6 네가 헬멧을 쓰면 안전할 것이다.

→ You (will / would) stay safe if you wear a helmet.

7 그들이 질문을 하면, 내가 대답할 수 있을 텐데.

→ If they (ask / asked) questions, I could answer them.

8 내가 채소를 먹으면, 건강을 유지할 텐데.

→ If I (eat / ate) vegetables, I would stay healthy.

9 그 거북이에게 날개가 있다면, 경주에서 이길 텐데.

→ If the turtle (has / had) wings, it would win the race.

10 그들이 규칙적으로 운동하면, 강해질 텐데.

→ If they exercised regularly, they (will / would) get strong.

11 우리가 더 열심히 훈련하면 경주에서 이길 수도 있을 텐데.

→ We (can / could) win the race if we trained harder.

12 우리가 열심히 일하면, 보상을 받을 텐데.

→ If we worked hard, we (will / would) get rewarded.

C 다음 우리말에 맞도록 괄호 안의 단어를 이용하여 빈칸에 알맞은 단어를 쓰시오.

1 내가 아프지 않았더라면, 나는 거기에 갔었을 텐데. (be)

→ If I ____________ ____________ ____________ ill, I would have gone there.

2 내가 사진을 찍었더라면, 나는 네게 보여 줄 수 있었을 텐데. (take)

→ If I ____________ ____________ the photo, I could have shown you.

3 그가 자켓을 입었더라면, 그는 추위를 느끼지 않았을 텐데. (wear)

→ If he ____________ ____________ a jacket, he wouldn't have felt cold.

4 그가 넘어지지 않았더라면, 그는 공을 잡을 수 있었을 텐데. (fall)

→ If he ____________ ____________ ____________ down, he could have caught the ball.

5 그가 그것을 했더라면, 그는 아프지 않았을 텐데. (do)

→ If he ____________ ____________ it, he wouldn't have been sick.

6 그녀가 열쇠를 찾았더라면, 그녀는 문을 열 수 있었을 텐데. (find)

→ If she ____________ ____________ the key, she could have opened the door.

7 내가 더 조심했더라면, 나는 사고를 피할 수 있었을 텐데. (avoid)

→ If I had been more careful, I ____________ ____________ ____________ the accident.

8 비가 오지 않았더라면, 우리는 소풍을 갔었을 텐데. (go)

→ If it had not rained, we ____________ ____________ ____________ on a picnic.

9 내가 그 사실을 알았더라면, 나는 당신에게 말해줬을 텐데. (tell)

→ If I had known the fact, I ____________ ____________ ____________ you.

10 내가 당신의 조언을 따랐더라면, 나는 성공할 수 있었을 텐데. (be)

→ If I had taken your advice, I ____________ ____________ ____________ successful.

11 당신이 나를 도와주지 않았더라면, 나는 실패했었을 텐데. (fail)

→ If you had not helped me, I ____________ ____________ ____________ .

12 내가 아침을 먹었더라면, 나는 그렇게 배고프지 않았을 텐데. (not, be)

→ If I had eaten breakfast, I ____________ ____________ ____________ ____________ so hungry.

 다음 대화의 괄호 안에서 알맞은 것을 고르시오.

1 A: Wow, it's such a nice day. I wish I (had / have) a bike.
   B: Right. If you had a bike, we (can / could) ride along the river today.

2 A: I wish it (is / were) sunny today.
   B: Yeah, if it (doesn't / didn't) rain, we could go outside.

3 A: My phone is broken. I wish I (had / have) a new one.
   B: Same here. If I (have / had) the money, I could buy one.

4 A: Ugh, I slept in again. I wish I (set / had set) the alarm last night.
   B: If you (set / had set) it, you wouldn't have missed the bus.

5 A: The club looks fun. I wish I (join / had joined) the club.
   B: Yeah, if you (join / had joined), you could have had fun, too.

6 A: Look at her. She looks as if she (is / were) sad.
   B: Yeah, I wish I (know / knew) what happened.

7 A: She talks as if she (owns / owned) the whole building.
   B: Yeah, I wish I (had / had had) that kind of confidence.

8 A: Look at Emma. She smiles as if she (didn't / doesn't) care.
   B: Yeah, I wish she (talks / talked) to us about how she really feels.

9 A: Is Kevin all right? He coughs as if he (was / had been) sick.
   B: Yeah, if I were him, I would (stay / have stayed) home.

10 A: She looks so tired. She sits as if she (walked / had walked) all day.
    B: Yeah, if I (am / were) her, I'd take a nap right now.

A 다음 우리말에 맞도록 괄호 안의 단어를 이용하여 빈칸에 알맞은 단어를 쓰시오.

1 Sam은 저녁 식사가 시작되기 전에 손을 씻었었다. (wash)

→ Sam ___________ ___________ his hands before dinner began.

2 우리는 수업이 시작되기 전에 점심을 먹었었다. (eat)

→ We ___________ ___________ lunch before the class started.

3 Anna는 시험이 시작되기 전에 복습을 끝냈었다. (finish)

→ Anna ___________ ______________ the review before the test began.

4 Jake는 겨울이 오기 전에 그 재킷을 사 두었었다. (buy)

→ Jake ___________ ___________ the jacket before the winter came.

5 택시가 도착했을 때 나는 가방을 싸지 않았었다. (not, pack)

→ I ___________ ___________ my bag when the taxi arrived.

6 가방을 열었을 때, 나는 지갑을 잃어버렸다는 것을 깨달았다. (lose)

→ Opening my bag, I realized I ___________ ___________ my wallet.

7 Tom은 그 영화를 보기 전에는 그 책을 읽지 않았다. (not, read)

→ Tom ___________ ___________ the book before he saw the movie.

8 우리는 버스를 놓쳐서, 학교까지 걸어갔다. (miss)

→ We ___________ ___________ the bus, so we walked to school.

9 그녀는 시험이 시작되기 전에 점심을 먹지 않았었다. (not, eat)

→ She ___________ ___________ lunch before the test began.

10 우리는 회의가 시작되기 전에 그를 만난 적이 없었다. (not, meet)

→ We ___________ ___________ him before the meeting started.

11 그 노래를 연습했던 학생들은 자신 있게 노래했다. (practice)

→ The students who ___________ ______________ the song sang confidently.

12 가방을 도둑맞은 그 소년은 걱정스러워 보였다. (steal)

→ The boy whose bag ___________ ___________ ___________ looked worried.

1 If he (is / were) here, he would help us.

2 If we (are / were) kind, we could make others happy.

3 If she (knows / knew) the answer, she would tell us.

4 If I (am / were) tall, I would play basketball well.

5 If she had a car, she (will / would) drive to school.

6 If I had enough money, I (will / would) buy a bicycle.

7 If they exercise regularly, they (will / would) get stronger.

8 They will be poor soon if they (spend / spent) too much.

9 If I turned off the light, I would (save / saves) electricity.

10 If she followed the rules, she would (avoid / avoids) trouble.

11 If my brother (takes / took) a taxi, he would arrive on time.

12 If they knew her phone number, they (call / would call) her.

13 If he (is / were) brave, he would speak in front of the class.

14 If they don't drink water, they (will / would) get thirsty soon.

15 You can't stay healthy if you (don't / didn't) eat vegetables.

16 If you heat water, it (will / would) boil very quickly.

17 If anyone studies, the person (will / would) get good grades.

18 The team will win the game if he (joins / joined) the team.

19 If they listened carefully, they (can / could) understand it easily.

20 If the team (practices / practiced) every day, they will improve quickly.

C 다음 밑줄 친 부분 중 어법상 <u>틀린</u> 곳을 찾아 바르게 고치시오.

1 My brother will win the race <u>if my brother ran</u>.

＿＿＿＿＿＿＿＿＿＿ → ＿＿＿＿＿＿＿＿＿＿

2 He will arrive on time <u>if he woke up early</u>.

＿＿＿＿＿＿＿＿＿＿ → ＿＿＿＿＿＿＿＿＿＿

3 <u>I understood it</u> if I watch the tutorial.

＿＿＿＿＿＿＿＿＿＿ → ＿＿＿＿＿＿＿＿＿＿

4 If I had wings, <u>I will fly to school</u>.

＿＿＿＿＿＿＿＿＿＿ → ＿＿＿＿＿＿＿＿＿＿

5 If she were a bird, <u>she will sing all day</u>.

＿＿＿＿＿＿＿＿＿＿ → ＿＿＿＿＿＿＿＿＿＿

6 If we lived in the mountains, <u>we can hike every weekend</u>.

＿＿＿＿＿＿＿＿＿＿ → ＿＿＿＿＿＿＿＿＿＿

7 <u>If he know the rules</u>, he would play the game better.

＿＿＿＿＿＿＿＿＿＿ → ＿＿＿＿＿＿＿＿＿＿

8 <u>If you have told me the truth</u>, I wouldn't have been angry.

＿＿＿＿＿＿＿＿＿＿ → ＿＿＿＿＿＿＿＿＿＿

9 <u>If we have studied together</u>, we would have learned a lot.

＿＿＿＿＿＿＿＿＿＿ → ＿＿＿＿＿＿＿＿＿＿

10 If the weather had been fine, <u>we would watch the stars at night</u>.

＿＿＿＿＿＿＿＿＿＿ → ＿＿＿＿＿＿＿＿＿＿

11 If she had walked faster, <u>she wouldn't have be late</u>.

＿＿＿＿＿＿＿＿＿＿ → ＿＿＿＿＿＿＿＿＿＿

12 <u>If we had took a taxi</u>, we would have arrived on time.

＿＿＿＿＿＿＿＿＿＿ → ＿＿＿＿＿＿＿＿＿＿

13 <u>If they have helped me</u>, I would have finished earlier.

＿＿＿＿＿＿＿＿＿＿ → ＿＿＿＿＿＿＿＿＿＿

14 <u>If I had know your address</u>, I would have visited you.

＿＿＿＿＿＿＿＿＿＿ → ＿＿＿＿＿＿＿＿＿＿

15 I am so tired today. If I were a cat, <u>I will sleep all day</u>.

＿＿＿＿＿＿＿＿＿＿ → ＿＿＿＿＿＿＿＿＿＿

 다음 괄호 안의 단어들을 바르게 배열하시오.

1 (I / could / wish / sing well / I / .)

→ ______________________________

2 (I / were / math / wish / good at / I / .)

→ ______________________________

3 (I / had / wish / I / many friends / .)

→ ______________________________

4 (I / didn't / I / have / wish / homework / .)

→ ______________________________

5 (I / not / wish / I / had / my wallet / lost / .)

→ ______________________________

6 (they / as if / were / run / they / athletes / .)

→ ______________________________

7 (he / were / as if / dances / he / on TV / .)

→ ______________________________

8 (she / as if / sings / she / a star / were / .)

→ ______________________________

E **다음 문장을 우리말로 해석하시오.**

1 I wish I had gone to the concert.

→ ______________________________

2 He plays the game as if it were real.

→ ______________________________

3 I wish I had taken many pictures.

→ ______________________________

4 I wish I had not eaten so much.

→ ______________________________

5 She smiles as if she had no worries.

→ ______________________________

[1-2] 다음 중 빈칸에 들어갈 말로 가장 적절한 것을 고르시오.

1

Lena _________ enough food before the guests arrived.

① cooks ② will cook
③ is cooking ④ has cooked
⑤ had cooked

2

Tom _________ his homework before his friends came over.

① does ② will do
③ is doing ④ has done
⑤ had done

3 다음 대화의 빈칸에 들어갈 말이 바르게 짝지어진 것은?

A: Why _________ Kevin enjoy the ride at the amusement park?
B: He _________ too much before he came, so he felt sick during the ride.

① didn't - has been eating
② didn't - has eaten
③ didn't - had eaten
④ doesn't - has eaten
⑤ doesn't - have eaten

4 다음 중 어법상 <u>틀린</u> 것은?

① He has never been to Japan.
② I have lived in this town since 2010.
③ She has already finished her homework.
④ We have arrived at the station before the train left.
⑤ They had already cleaned the room when their mom arrived.

[5-6] 다음 우리말에 맞도록 빈칸에 알맞은 말을 쓰시오.

5

앨리스가 두고 간 가방이 교실에서 발견되었다.

→ The bag that Alice ___________ ___________ was found in the classroom.

6

그 고양이는 마치 모든 게 자기 것인 것처럼 방을 돌아다녔다.

→ The cat walked around the room ____________ it owned everything.

7 다음 중 올바른 가정법 문장은?

① He will have helped us if we had asked.

② I would go to the party if I had been invited.

③ We would help her if she had worked harder.

④ She would have finished earlier if she studies harder.

⑤ They would have helped us if they had known the situation.

[8-10] 다음 문장의 의미와 같은 것을 고르시오.

8

I can't go outside because it's raining.

① I will go outside if it rains.

② I could go outside if it weren't raining.

③ I don't want to go outside because it is raining.

④ I could have gone outside if it had stopped raining.

⑤ I want to go outside because it is not raining.

9

I couldn't join the trip because I forgot to apply.

① If I apply, I can join the trip.

② If I applied early, I would join the trip.

③ If I don't forget to apply, I will join the trip.

④ If I didn't forget to apply, I could join the trip.

⑤ If I hadn't forgotten to apply, I would have joined the trip.

10

I'm not tall, so I can't reach the top shelf.

① I act as if I can reach the top shelf.

② I'm not sure if I can reach the top shelf.

③ I am sure that I am tall enough to reach the top shelf.

④ I wish I were tall enough to reach the top shelf.

⑤ I wished I were tall enough to reach the top shelf.

[11-12] 다음 밑줄 친 부분에서 어법상 <u>틀린</u> 곳을 찾아 바르게 고치시오.

11

We might have won the game if <u>we played together</u>.

__________________ → __________________

12

If I have turned off the oven, the cookies wouldn't have burned.

__________________ → __________________

[13-15] 다음 우리말에 맞도록 빈칸에 알맞은 말을 **보기** 에서 골라 쓰시오.

보기 have had been wouldn't have

13

고양이가 안에 머물렀더라면, 젖지 않았을 텐데.

→ If the cat had stayed inside, it
_______________ gotten wet.

14

그녀가 운이 좋았더라면, 그 상을 탔을 텐데.

→ If she had _______________ lucky, she
would _______________ won the prize.

15

그녀가 카메라를 가지고 있었더라면, 사진을
찍을 수 있었을 텐데.

→ If she had _______________ a camera, she
could have taken pictures.

[16-17] 다음 우리말에 맞도록 괄호 안의 단어들을
바르게 배열하시오.

16

Jim은 마치 그 책을 읽었던 것처럼 말한다.
(had / if / Jim / as / he / read / talks /
the book / .)

→ _________________________________

17

Katie는 마치 레슨을 받았던 것처럼 노래한다.
(she / if / Katie / as / had / sings /
lessons / taken / .)

→ _________________________________

[18-19] 다음 문장을 I wish 가정법으로 바꿔 문장을
완성하시오.

18

I'm sorry that we don't have PE class today.

→ I wish _________________________.

19

I'm sorry that I didn't bring my umbrella.

→ I wish ___________________________

___________________________.

22 다음 중 어법상 옳은 문장을 모두 고르면?

① I wish she knows how to swim.

② He talks as if he were the president.

③ If they have time, they would help us.

④ If I were a bird, I would fly in the sky.

⑤ If she has invited me, I would have gone to the party.

[20-21] **다음 대화에서 어법상 틀린 곳을 찾아 바르게 고치시오.**

20

A: If I had more free time, I would travel the world.
B: You're right. If I also had enough money, I will visit Italy.

___________________ → ___________________

23 다음 글의 밑줄 친 부분 중 어법상 옳은 것끼리 바르게 짝지어진 것은?

We didn't go to Paris last winter. I wish we ⓐhad gone there. My friend talks as if he ⓑhad been to Paris, but he didn't go. If we had been in Paris, we could ⓒhave seen the Eiffel Tower. If I ⓓam rich, I would travel the world one day.

21

A: I wish I were tall enough to play basketball well.
B: Same here. If I am tall, I would join the school team.

___________________ → ___________________

① ⓐ

② ⓐ, ⓑ

③ ⓐ, ⓑ, ⓒ

④ ⓐ, ⓒ, ⓓ

⑤ ⓑ, ⓒ, ⓓ

5

접속사

- 명사절을 이끄는 접속사
- 부사절을 이끄는 접속사
- 상관접속사
- 접속부사

명사절을 이끄는 접속사

접속사	의미	예문 / 역할
		문장이 주어, 목적어, 보어 역할을 할 수 있도록 명사로 바꿔 주는 접속사
that	~라는 것	That she is kind is true. (주어절) = It is true that she is kind. (가주어, 진주어) I think that he is honest. (목적어절) The problem is that we don't have enough time. (보어절)
whether / if	~인지 아닌지	Whether he will come is not certain. (주어절) I don't know if she likes pizza. (목적어절) The issue is whether or not he told the truth. (보어절) *whether or not (O), if or not (X)

A 다음 문장에서 접속사를 포함한 명사절에 밑줄 치시오.

1 I heard that you moved to a new school.

2 Whether you join us or not is your choice.

부사절을 이끄는 접속사

접속사	뜻	예문
when	~할 때	When I got home, it was dark.
while	~하는 동안	While she was cooking, he set the table.
as	~하면서, ~할 때	As he walked, he listened to music.
before	~하기 전에	Before you eat, wash your hands.
after	~한 후에	After he finished his homework, he played games.
because, since	~때문에	We're late because the bus didn't come.
so that, in order that	~하기 위해서, ~하도록	I spoke slowly so that everyone could understand me.
although, even though	비록 ~이지만	Although he was tired, he kept working.
even if	만약 ~일지라도	Even if she calls, I won't answer.

B 다음 우리말에 맞도록 괄호 안에서 알맞은 것을 고르시오.

1 우리는 쇼핑을 끝낸 후 카페에 머물렀다.

→ We stayed at the café (after / before) we finished shopping.

2 비록 그녀는 피곤했지만, 계속 공부했다.

→ (When / Although) she was tired, she kept studying.

두 개의 단어나 구, 절을 짝지어 연결해 주는 접속사		
상관접속사 구조	뜻	예문
both A and B	A와 B 둘 다	Both the dog and the cat are sleeping.
either A or B	A 또는 B 둘 중 하나	Either you or your brother must go.
neither A nor B	A도 B도 아닌	Neither my phone nor my tablet is working.
not only A but also B	A뿐만 아니라 B도	She is not only smart but also very kind.

C 다음 괄호 안에서 알맞은 것을 고르시오.

1   I like both pizza (or / and) pasta.

2   I will bring either cookies (or / and) cake for the picnic.

3   She is not only a good singer but (nor / also) a great dancer.

두 문장을 연결하고, 두 문장간의 관계를 보여 주는 부사			
대조	however (하지만) in contrast (대조적으로)	결과	therefore, thus (그러므로) as a result (결과적으로)
첨가	besides, moreover, furthermore (게다가)	화제 전환	by the way (그런데)
양보	nevertheless (그럼에도 불구하고)	요약	in short (요약하면)
예시	for example, for instance (예를 들면)	비교	similarly (비슷하게) likewise (마찬가지로)

예문:
- My brother likes action movies. In contrast, I prefer comedies.
- The book is interesting. Moreover, it teaches good lessons.

D 다음 괄호 안에서 알맞은 것을 고르시오.

1   I studied hard. (However / Therefore), I didn't get a good grade.

2   He failed the test. (Thus / Nevertheless), he didn't give up.

A 다음 밑줄 친 부분이 주어절, 목적어절, 보어절 중 어느 것에 해당하는지 고르시오.

1 <u>That she won the prize</u> made her parents proud. (주어 / 목적어 / 보어)

2 I heard <u>that she moved to Canada</u>. (주어 / 목적어 / 보어)

3 The fact is <u>that we can't change the past</u>. (주어 / 목적어 / 보어)

4 The reason is <u>that they misunderstood the rules</u>. (주어 / 목적어 / 보어)

5 <u>Whether we win or lose</u> doesn't matter. (주어 / 목적어 / 보어)

6 The question is <u>whether they can finish on time</u>. (주어 / 목적어 / 보어)

7 She wants to know <u>if you enjoyed the movie</u>. (주어 / 목적어 / 보어)

8 The big question is <u>whether they support our plan</u>. (주어 / 목적어 / 보어)

B 다음 우리말에 맞도록 빈칸에 알맞은 말을 보기 에서 골라 쓰시오.

| 보기 | although | while | when | because | before |

1 벨이 울렸을 때, 모두가 조용해졌다.
→ ______________ the bell rang, everyone became quiet.

2 그는 버스를 기다리는 동안에, 영어 단어를 외웠다.
→ ______________ he was waiting for the bus, he memorized English words.

3 네가 안전벨트를 매기 전에, 차를 출발시키면 안 된다.
→ ______________ you fasten your seat belt, you must not start the car.

4 비가 오고 있었기 때문에, 나는 장화를 신었다.
→ ______________ it was raining, I wore my rain boots.

5 비록 그는 시험에 합격했지만, 행복하지 않았다.
→ ______________ he passed the test, he didn't feel happy.

 다음 괄호 안에서 알맞은 것을 고르시오.

1 I have visited both Paris (or / and) Rome.

2 You can wear either sneakers (or / and) sandals for the trip.

3 She owns neither a smartphone (or / nor) a laptop.

4 He is not only a talented artist but (nor / also) a skilled photographer.

5 You can join either the chess club (or / and) the drama club.

6 They faced neither strong winds (or / nor) heavy rain on their journey.

7 The library has both English (or / and) Korean books.

8 This app is not only easy to use but (nor / also) completely free.

D 다음 우리말에 맞도록 빈칸에 알맞은 말을 보기 에서 골라 쓰시오.

보기 therefore   however   for example   likewise   nevertheless

1 나는 여행을 가고 싶었다. 하지만, 비행기 표가 너무 비쌌다.
   → I wanted to travel. __________________, the plane tickets were too expensive.

2 그는 시험공부를 열심히 했다. 그래서, 좋은 성적을 받았다.
   → He studied hard for the exam. __________________, he got a good grade.

3 비가 많이 왔다. 그럼에도 불구하고, 우리는 야외 콘서트를 즐겼다.
   → It rained heavily. __________________, we enjoyed the outdoor concert.

4 이 도시에는 다양한 종류의 길거리 음식이 있다. 예를 들어, 매운 떡볶이가 유명하다.
   → This city has many kinds of street food. __________________, the spicy tteokbokki is popular.

5 내 남동생은 피아노를 배운다. 마찬가지로, 나는 바이올린을 배운다.
   → My younger brother learns the piano. __________________, I learn the violin.

A 다음 괄호 안에서 알맞은 것을 고르시오.

1 I know (who / that) she is a great singer.

2 He believes (that / which) the plan will work.

3 She asked (which / whether) they were ready to start.

4 She mentioned (what / that) she would be late.

5 It is true (that / which) exercise is good for your health.

6 She explained (what / that) she had finished the project.

7 I can't decide (that / whether) I should join the club or not.

8 (That / Which) he forgot my birthday hurt my feelings.

9 They agreed (what / that) the meeting should be put off.

10 I hope (what / that) you enjoy your vacation.

11 We discovered (what / that) the shop was closed.

12 They will check (if / which) the package has arrived.

13 (That / Which) we have no school tomorrow makes me happy.

14 (Which / Whether) the store opens tomorrow hasn't been decided.

15 The fact is (that / which) nobody knows the answer.

16 He doubts (which / whether) the story is real or not.

17 (What / Whether) the rumor is true remains a mystery.

18 I wonder (if / which) he has finished the report.

19 It is strange (what / that) he didn't answer my calls.

20 My only question is (what / whether) you are ready for the test.

1 그가 기타를 연주하는 동안에, 그의 친구들은 노래를 불렀다.

→ (While / Because) he played the guitar, his friends sang along.

2 버스가 정류장에 도착하자, 승객들이 서둘러 내렸다.

→ (As / Although) the bus arrived at the stop, the passengers hurried to get off.

3 영화를 보고 나서, 우리는 근처 카페에 갔다.

→ (Before / After) we watched the movie, we went to a nearby café.

4 눈이 많이 내렸기 때문에, 학교가 하루 휴교했다.

→ (When / Because) it snowed a lot, the school was closed for a day.

5 그녀는 몸이 아팠지만, 수업에 끝까지 참여했다.

→ (When / Although) she was sick, she stayed in class until the end.

6 비록 연습 시간이 부족했지만, 그는 훌륭하게 연주했다.

→ (As / Even though) he had little practice time, he performed wonderfully.

7 회의가 시작되기 전에, 자료를 모두 나누어 주어라.

→ (Before / After) the meeting starts, please hand out all the materials.

8 부모님이 외출하신 동안에, 우리는 방을 청소했다.

→ (While / Because) our parents were out, we cleaned our room.

9 비록 그 영화는 매우 길었지만, 놀랍게도 지루하지 않았다.

→ (As / Although) the movie was very long, it was surprisingly not boring.

10 비록 늦게 도착했지만, 우리는 공연을 거의 다 볼 수 있었다.

→ (Since / Even though) we arrived late, we could watch most of the show.

11 종이 울렸을 때, 학생들은 운동장으로 나갔다.

→ (When / Because) the bell rang, the students went out to the playground.

12 마지막 손님이 나간 후에, 불이 갑자기 꺼졌다.

→ (After / Before) the last guest left, the lights suddenly turned off.

13 친구를 만나기 위해 나는 일찍 떠났다.

→ I left early (so that / because) I could meet my friend.

14 설령 사람들이 그녀를 의심하더라도, 그녀는 자신의 아이디어를 발표할 것이다.

→ (Whether / Even if) people doubt her, she will present her idea.

15 시험에 합격하기 위해 그녀는 열심히 공부한다.

→ She studies hard in order (to / that) she will pass the exam.

C 다음 괄호 안에서 알맞은 것을 고르시오.

1   Both my sister (or / and) my brother like playing basketball.

2   You can have either coffee (or / and) tea after dinner.

3   Neither my mom (or / nor) my dad can pick me up today.

4   Not only the weather but (also / too) the food was perfect.

5   We visited both the museum (or / and) the art gallery on our trip.

6   We can meet either at the library (or / and) at the café.

7   She is neither interested (or / nor) motivated to join the club.

8   The movie was not (only / that) exciting but also very funny.

9   (Both / Either) the bus stop and the subway station are crowded.

10   She is (both / either) smart and kind to everyone.

11   He will be (either / neither) tired or hungry after the long game.

12   They have (either / neither) time nor money to travel this year.

13   He speaks not only English (but / and) also French fluently.

14   You can choose either chocolate cake (or / and) ice cream for dessert.

15   (Either / Neither) my friends nor my family knows about the surprise.

16   The restaurant serves not only food (but / and) also fresh drinks.

17   My cousins are (both / either) funny and friendly.

18   I will bring either sandwiches (or / and) fruit for the picnic.

19   The package was neither big (or / nor) heavy.

20   The park is not (also / only) beautiful but also peaceful in the morning.

 다음 대화의 괄호 안에서 알맞은 것을 고르시오.

1 A: I thought the math test would be easy.

 B: I studied a lot. (However / Whenever), it was much harder than I expected.

2 A: I reviewed all my notes and solved every problem.

 B: You really worked hard. (Therefore / For example), you'll get a good result.

3 A: I enjoy painting after school.

 B: It's very relaxing. (Moreover / However), it helps you express your feelings.

4 A: The bus broke down on the way to school.

 B: We had to wait in the cold. (Thus / Similarly), many students arrived late.

5 A: We forgot to lock the window last night.

 B: A strong wind blew in. (Likewise / Nevertheless), nothing in the room was damaged.

6 A: Does your dad enjoy outdoor activities?

 B: He spends a lot of time in nature. (For example / In contrast), he goes fishing almost every weekend.

7 A: I think walking to school is good for you.

 B: It also helps the environment. (Furthermore / For instance), it saves money on bus fares.

8 A: You forgot to set your alarm last night.

 B: I woke up late. (In contrast / As a result), I missed the first class.

9 A: I saw your sister at the park yesterday.

 B: She was walking her dog. (By the way / On the way), how is your family doing?

A 다음 우리말에 맞도록 빈칸에 알맞은 말을 쓰시오.

1 나는 네가 시험에 합격했다는 것을 들었다.

→ I heard _______________ you passed the exam.

2 우리는 그가 영어를 잘한다는 것을 알고 있다.

→ We know _______________ he is good at English.

3 그는 내가 초대를 받았는지 물어봤다.

→ He asked _______________ I had received the invitation.

4 그녀는 내가 그의 이름을 기억하는지 확인했다.

→ She checked _______________ I remembered his name.

5 우리는 그들이 그 계획에 동의했다는 것을 들었다.

→ We heard _______________ they agreed on the plan.

6 나는 네가 나를 도와줬다는 것에 정말로 감사한다.

→ I really appreciate _______________ you helped me.

7 나는 네가 그 소식을 들었을 것이라고 믿는다.

→ I believe _______________ you heard the news.

8 그는 내가 숙제를 끝냈는지 궁금해했다.

→ He wondered _______________ I had finished the homework.

9 그는 그 질문이 어렵다는 것을 이해했다.

→ He understood _______________ the question was difficult.

10 우리는 그가 새로운 취미를 시작했다는 것을 알았다.

→ We learned _______________ he started a new hobby.

11 그녀는 내가 약속을 지켰다는 것을 인정했다.

→ She admitted _______________ I kept my promise.

12 기자는 그 소문이 사실인지 확인했다.

→ The reporter checked _______________ the rumor was true.

B 다음 우리말에 맞도록 빈칸에 알맞은 말을 보기 에서 골라 쓰시오.

보기 while   because   when   so that   although   before   after

1 네가 도착했을 때, 나는 저녁을 요리하고 있었다.

→ ________________ you arrived, I was cooking dinner.

2 그는 휴대폰을 사용하고 있는 동안, 음악을 듣고 있었다.

→ ________________ he was using his phone, he was listening to music.

3 그녀는 떠나기 전에, 창문을 닫았다.

→ ________________ she left, she closed the window.

4 나는 배가 고팠기 때문에, 샌드위치를 만들었다.

→ ________________ I was hungry, I made a sandwich.

5 손님들이 편히 앉도록 우리는 의자를 더 가지고 왔다.

→ We brought more chairs ________________ the guests could sit comfortably.

6 날씨가 추웠지만, 아이들은 밖에서 놀았다.

→ ________________ it was cold, the children played outside.

7 나는 책을 다 읽고 나서 잠자리에 늘었다.

→ I went to bed ________________ I finished reading the book.

8 그가 열심히 공부했기 때문에, 그는 좋은 점수를 받았다.

→ ________________ he studied hard, he got a good score.

9 그녀는 높은 구두를 신었지만 빨리 걸었다.

→ ________________ she wore high heels, she walked fast.

10 나는 문제가 생겼을 때, 친구에게 도움을 요청했다.

→ ________________ I had a problem, I asked my friend for help.

11 비록 그는 운전면허가 있었지만, 버스를 타고 출근했다.

→ ________________ he had a driver's license, he took the bus to work.

12 그는 모든 사람이 들을 수 있도록, 목소리를 높였다.

→ He raised his voice ________________ everyone could hear.

C 다음 우리말에 맞도록 괄호 안의 단어들을 바르게 배열하시오.

1 그녀는 영어와 일본어 둘 다 할 수 있다.
(can / both / and / speak / she / English / Japanese / .)

→ ____

2 너는 버스나 지하철 중 하나를 탈 수 있다.
(the bus / take / you / either / can / the subway / or / .)

→ ____

3 그는 수영도 달리기도 잘 못한다.
(is / a good swimmer / he / neither / nor / a good runner / .)

→ ____

4 그는 친절할 뿐 아니라 똑똑하다.
(is / not only / he / but also / kind / smart / .)

→ ____

5 그는 피자나 햄버거 중 하나를 원한다.
(wants / the pizza / he / the hamburger / or / either / .)

→ ____

6 그녀는 노래뿐 아니라 춤도 춘다.
(dances / she / sings / not only / but also / .)

→ ____

7 나는 그 영화도 그 책도 좋아하지 않는다.
(like / neither / I / nor / the book / the movie / .)

→ ____

8 나는 수학 선생님과 영어 선생님 두 분 모두 존경한다.
(my math teacher / respect / I / and / my English teacher / both / .)

→ ____

9 그녀는 그림을 그릴 뿐 아니라 노래도 할 수 있다.
(can / but also / not only / she / paint / sing / .)

→ ____

10 너는 샐러드나 스프 중 하나를 주문할 수 있다.
(order / a salad / either / can / soup / or / you / .)

→ ____

D 다음 우리말에 맞도록 괄호 안의 단어들을 바르게 배열하시오.

1 나는 열심히 공부했다. 하지만, 시험은 어려웠다.
(studied / however, / was / I / the test / hard / difficult / . / .)

→ ______________________________________

2 비가 많이 왔다. 결과적으로, 경기가 취소되었다.
(rained / it / a lot / as a result, / canceled / was / the game / . / .)

→ ______________________________________

3 그 책은 재미있다. 게다가, 그것은 유익하다.
(is / moreover, / the book / it / interesting / useful / is / . / .)

→ ______________________________________

4 그는 피곤했다. 그럼에도 불구하고, 그는 계속 달렸다.
(nevertheless, / he / tired / was / he / running / kept / . / .)

→ ______________________________________

5 그는 항상 연습했다. 그러므로, 그는 경연에서 우승했다.
(practiced / he / always / therefore, / won / he / the contest / . / .)

→ ______________________________________

6 날씨가 좋네. 그런데, 네 계획은 뭐니?
(are / the weather / nice / by the way, / what / is / plans / your / . / ?)

→ ______________________________________

7 그는 숙제를 끝냈다. 게다가, 그는 방 청소도 했다.
(besides, / he / cleaned / finished / the room / his homework / also / he / . / .)

→ ______________________________________

8 버스가 지연되었다. 그러므로, 우리는 늦었다.
(was / thus, / the bus / late / delayed / were / we / . / .)

→ ______________________________________

9 그의 방은 깨끗하다. 대조적으로, 그의 형 방은 지저분하다.
(messy / is / his brother's room / in contrast, / his room / clean / is / . / .)

→ ______________________________________

10 그는 규칙적으로 운동했다. 그 결과, 그의 건강이 좋아졌다.
(he / exercised / improved / as a result, / his health / regularly / . / .)

→ ______________________________________

1 다음 중 밑줄 친 **that**이 접속사로 쓰이지 <u>않은</u> 것은?

① She said <u>that</u> she was busy.

② I know <u>that</u> they are coming.

③ She hopes <u>that</u> you enjoy the trip.

④ The boy <u>that</u> is playing soccer is my cousin.

⑤ I heard <u>that</u> the weather will be nice tomorrow.

2 다음 중 밑줄 친 부분이 목적어 역할을 하지 <u>않는</u> 것은?

① He thinks <u>that the movie is interesting</u>.

② She explained <u>that the bus was late</u>.

③ I remember <u>that he visited us last year</u>.

④ They understand <u>that the rules are important</u>.

⑤ The problem is <u>that we don't have enough time</u>.

[3-6] 다음 우리말에 맞도록 빈칸에 들어갈 말로 가장 적절한 것을 고르시오.

3

내가 책을 읽고 있을 때, 친구가 나에게 전화를 했다.
→ __________ I was reading a book, my friend called me.

① Because   ② Although

③ Even though   ④ When

⑤ Since

4

나는 피곤했기 때문에, 일찍 잠자리에 들었다.
→ __________ I was tired, I went to bed early.

① Because   ② After

③ When   ④ While

⑤ Although

5

비록 나는 긴장했지만, 발표 동안 또렷하게 말했다.
→ __________ I was nervous, I spoke clearly during the presentation.

① Since   ② After

③ When   ④ As

⑤ Although

6

모든 사람이 그 규칙을 이해하도록 내가 다시 그것을 설명할 것이다.
→ I will explain it again __________ everyone understands the rule.

① even though   ② because

③ although   ④ so that

⑤ after

보기　　nor　　　but　　　and

7

그들은 친절하고 정직하다.

→ They are both kind _________ honest.

8

그 영화는 무섭지도 않고 웃기지도 않았다.

→ The movie was neither scary _________ funny.

9

그 팀은 경기에서 이겼을 뿐만 아니라 신기록도 세웠다.

→ The team not only won the game _________ also set a new record.

[10-11] 다음 문장에서 어법상 **틀린** 곳을 찾아 바르게 고치시오.

10

We need either a map nor a guide for the trip .

_________________ → _________________

11

The task requires not only teamwork not also creative thinking.

_________________ → _________________

12 다음 글의 밑줄 친 부분 중 어법상 **틀린** 것은?

Sarah went camping in the mountains ①because she wanted to take a break from work. She thought ②that she would be back before the sunset. ③While she was walking along the trail, she enjoyed the sound of birds singing. At the campsite, she could choose ④neither a spot near the river or one under the big oak tree. ⑤Even though it started to rain, she decided to stay.

①　　　②　　　③　　　④　　　⑤

[13-14] 다음 대화의 빈칸에 들어갈 말로 가장 적절한 것을 고르시오.

13

A: The café was crowded. Did you find a seat?
B: _________ it was full, I found a small table by the window.

① If ② After
③ Since ④ Because
⑤ Although

14

A: How was her speech?
B: She had practiced a lot. _________, she forgot some lines on stage.

① Nevertheless ② Therefore
③ Similarly ④ Because
⑤ For example

[15-17] 다음 우리말에 맞도록 빈칸에 알맞은 말을 쓰시오.

15

그녀는 보고서에 실수를 했다고 인정했다.

→ She admitted _____________ she had made a mistake in the report.

16

아무도 그가 말하는 것을 들을 수 없도록 그는 속삭였다.

→ He whispered ___________ ___________ no one else could hear him.

17

어제는 내 휴대폰도 태블릿도 작동하지 않았다.

→ Neither my phone _____________ my tablet worked yesterday.

18 다음 중 어법상 <u>틀린</u> 것은?

① I know that she likes painting.
② He is the man that he helped me.
③ We hope that you can join us.
④ That you are here makes me happy.
⑤ The idea is that we shouldn't work all night.

19

나는 책뿐만 아니라 잡지도 읽는다.
(read / I / not only / books / magazines / but also / .)

→ _______________________________________

20

우리는 환경을 보호해야 한다. 예를 들어, 우리는 플라스틱을 재활용할 수 있다.
(should / we / the environment / for instance, / protect / recycle / we / plastic / can / . / .)

→ _______________________________________

____

[21-22] 다음 대화의 빈칸에 들어갈 말이 바르게 짝지어진 것을 고르시오.

21

A: I need both a pen _________ a pencil for the test. Do you have them?
B: Sorry, I have neither a pen _________ a pencil. You can ask Tom.

① or - and

② and - or

③ and - nor

④ nor - and

⑤ but - nor

22

• A: I was sleepy in class. _________, I listened carefully to the teacher.
  B: Good job.
• A: I enjoy drawing. _________, my sister enjoys drawing, too.
  B: You can draw together.

① However - Nevertheless

② Therefore - Similarly

③ However - In contrast

④ Nevertheless - Likewise

⑤ In contrast - Nevertheless

23 다음 글에서 문맥상 자연스러운 것을 <u>모두</u> 고르면?

1. Hana likes painting pictures. ⓐSimilarly, she is often too busy.
2. She studies hard at school. ⓑFurthermore, she helps her friends study English.
3. She wanted better grades. ⓒNevertheless, she studied every night.
4. She loves animals. ⓓFor example, she takes care of a dog.
5. She is kind to her classmates. ⓔIn contrast, they are kind to her.

① ⓐ, ⓑ

② ⓑ, ⓒ

③ ⓑ, ⓓ

④ ⓐ, ⓑ, ⓓ

⑤ ⓑ, ⓓ, ⓔ

일치와 화법

수의 일치

표현	수 일치	표현	수 일치
each, every, -one, -thing, -body	단수	the number of ~ (~의 수), a number of ~ (많은 ~)	단수 복수
both A and B, the + 형용사	복수	one of the 복수명사, each of the 복수명사	단수
a lot of, lots of, plenty of + 명사	명사에 일치	all, most, none, half, rest, 분수, 퍼센트 + of 명사	명사에 일치
There is / are + 명사	명사에 일치	not A but B, either A or B, neither A nor B, not only A but also B, B as well as A	B에 일치
동명사구, to부정사구, 명사절(that절, 의문사절)	단수		

A 다음 괄호 안에서 알맞은 것을 고르시오.

1 One of the dogs (runs / run) to greet me.

2 A number of students (is / are) participating.

3 There (is / are) some books on the desk.

시제 일치

주절의 시제	종속절의 시제	예문
현재	모든 시제 (현재, 과거, 미래)	I know that she is happy. (현재) I know that she was happy yesterday. (과거)
과거	과거	He said that he was angry.
	과거 완료	He said that he had done his homework.
	현재시제 (예외)	He said that the Earth is round. (보편적 사실)

B 다음 빈칸에 들어갈 말로 적절한 것을 고르시오.

1 I thought that he ________ sick.

　① is　　　　② was　　　　③ will be

2 She said that she ________ her project.

　① finishes　　② will finish　　③ had finished

<table>
<tr><th colspan="2">평서문의 화법 전환</th></tr>
<tr><th>전환 방법</th><th>설명</th></tr>
<tr><td>① 전달 동사 변경</td><td>주절의 동사를 변경 (say → say / say to → tell)</td></tr>
<tr><td>② 기호 제거, 접속사 추가</td><td>주절의 콤마와 따옴표를 삭제하고 접속사 that 쓰기</td></tr>
<tr><td>③ 대명사, 시제, 부사 변경</td><td>종속절의 대명사, 동사, 부사를 시제와 문맥에 맞게 수정</td></tr>
</table>

예문:
* 직접화법: He said, "I will see her here tomorrow."
* 간접화법: He ① said ② that ③ he would see her there the next day.

* 지시대명사와 부사 전환
  - now → at that time(then)   - this / these → that / those   - yesterday → the day before
  - ago → before   - today → that day   - here → there   - tomorrow → the next day

C 다음 문장이 간접화법으로 알맞게 바뀌도록 괄호 안에서 알맞은 것을 고르시오.

1 Tom said, "I will eat lunch." → Tom said that (I / he) would eat lunch.

2 Anna said, "I can play the piano." → Anna said that she (can / could) play the piano.

<table>
<tr><th colspan="3">의문문과 명령문의 화법 전환 / 간접의문문</th></tr>
<tr><th>유형</th><th>전환 방법</th><th>예문</th></tr>
<tr><td rowspan="3">의문문의
화법 전환</td><td>① say, say to → ask</td><td rowspan="3">He said, "What time does the train leave?"
→ He ① asked ② what time the train ③ left.

He said, "Are you coming?"
→ He ① asked ② if ③ I was coming.</td></tr>
<tr><td>② 콤마, 따옴표 삭제 후 어순 변경
* 의문사 O: 「의문사 + 주어 + 동사」
* 의문사 X: 「If[Whether] + 주어 + 동사」</td></tr>
<tr><td>③ 대명사, 시제, 부사 변경</td></tr>
<tr><td rowspan="2">명령문의
화법 전환</td><td>① tell, ask, advise, order로 변경</td><td rowspan="2">She said to me, "Close the door."
→ She ① told me ② to close the door.</td></tr>
<tr><td>② 동사원형 → to부정사로 변경</td></tr>
<tr><th></th><th>예문</th><th>설명</th></tr>
<tr><td>간접의문문</td><td>Do you know? + Where is she?
→ Do you know where she is?</td><td>의문문이 문장 내에서 주어 / 목적어 / 보어의
역할을 할 때 「의문사 + 주어 + 동사」 어순으로 씀</td></tr>
</table>

D 다음 문장의 화법을 전환할 때 빈칸에 적절한 말을 쓰시오.

1 Mom said, "Are you sleeping?" → Mom ______________ if I was sleeping.

2 [I wonder] + [Who is the man?] → I wonder ______________________________.

A 다음 중 밑줄 친 부분이 어법상 옳으면 ○, 아니라면 X를 표시하시오.

1   Listening to music <u>is</u> fun.   (　)

2   A lot of water <u>are</u> needed.   (　)

3   Every dog <u>need</u> a home.   (　)

4   Lots of people <u>was</u> late.   (　)

5   Both you and I <u>like</u> soccer.   (　)

6   There <u>is</u> a cat on the roof.   (　)

7   The poor <u>needs</u> more support.   (　)

8   The number of students <u>are</u> growing. (　)

9   To draw pictures <u>make</u> me happy.   (　)

10 One of the apples <u>are</u> rotten.   (　)

B 다음 중 어법상 옳은 문장에는 ○, 틀린 문장에는 X를 표시하시오.

1   He said that he is tired.   (　)

2   I think that she liked pizza.   (　)

3   She told me that she sees the movie.   (　)

4   He believes that the Earth moves around the Sun.   (　)

5   They knew that the dog runs away.   (　)

6   I know that he plays soccer every weekend.   (　)

7   She said that she doesn't do her homework.   (　)

8   My teacher said that water boils at 100°C.   (　)

9   I realized that I had met him before.   (　)

10 He said that the sun rose in the east.   (　)

 다음 두 문장의 의미가 같도록 괄호 안에서 알맞은 것을 고르시오.

1 David said, "I have a cat."

= David said that (I / he) had a cat.

2 Emily said, "I must study."

= Emily said that she (has to / had to) study.

3 Sam said, "I'm happy."

= Sam said that (I'm / he was) happy.

4 Jack said, "I will go shopping."

= Jack said that he (went / would go) shopping.

5 Emma said, "I saw a rainbow."

= Emma said that she (saw / had seen) a rainbow.

D 다음 두 문장의 의미가 같도록 빈칸에 알맞은 말을 쓰시오.

1 She said to me, "Sit down."

= She told me ___________ sit down.

2 "Do you like bananas?" he said.

= He asked ___________ ___________ liked bananas.

3 The teacher said to me, "Open the book."

= The teacher ___________ me ___________ open the book.

4 He said, "What are you doing?"

= He asked ___________ ___________ ___________ doing.

5 He said, "How do you solve the problem?"

= He asked ___________ ___________ ___________ the problem.

6 "What time will you be home?" Mom said.

= Mom asked what time ___________ ___________ ___________ home.

A 다음 괄호 안에서 알맞은 것을 고르시오.

1 One of the boys (is / are) tall.

2 All of the water (is / are) gone.

3 Most of the cake (was / were) eaten.

4 Neither she nor they (is / are) ready.

5 The rich (has / have) a lot of wealth.

6 Each student (has / have) a workbook.

7 A lot of sugar (makes / make) desserts sweet.

8 Reading books (helps / help) me relax.

9 That the Earth is round (is / are) a fact.

10 There (is / are) a problem with the plan.

11 The young (enjoys / enjoy) playing games.

12 Both Tom and Jerry (is / are) in the room.

13 There (has / have) been several calls today.

14 30% of the people (supports / support) the law.

15 All of the boys who play soccer (is / are) tired.

16 Plenty of oranges (grow / grows) in that region.

17 A number of teachers (supports / support) the idea.

18 Each of the books that I read (was / were) interesting.

19 Not only the wolf but also the dogs (howls / howl) loudly.

20 The singer as well as the dancers (performs / perform) tonight.

1 나는 그녀가 피곤하다고 생각했다. (be)

→ I thought that she ___________ tired.

2 나는 그녀가 열심히 공부하고 있다고 생각한다. (study)

→ I think that she ___________ ___________ hard.

3 그는 출근 전에 자기 가방을 잃어버렸다고 말했다. (lose)

→ He said that he ___________ ___________ his bag before going to work.

4 나는 일부 사자들이 아프리카에 산다고 알고 있다. (live)

→ I know that some lions ___________ in Africa.

5 그녀는 저녁을 요리하고 있다고 말했다. (cook)

→ She said that she ___________ ___________ dinner.

6 나는 내일 비가 올 거라고 믿는다. (rain)

→ I believe that it ___________ ___________ tomorrow.

7 나는 그가 당근을 좋아하지 않는다는 것을 안다. (not, like)

→ I know that he ___________ ___________ carrots.

8 그는 저녁 식사 전에 창문을 깼다고 내게 말했다. (break)

→ He told me that he ___________ ___________ the window before dinner.

9 그들은 그 영화를 보지 않았다고 말했다. (not, see)

→ They said that they ___________ ___________ the movie.

10 엄마는 저녁이 준비되었다고 내게 말씀하셨다. (be)

→ My mom told me that dinner ___________ ready.

11 그는 막 점심을 다 먹었다고 내게 말했다. (just, finish)

→ He told me that he ___________ ___________ ___________ his lunch.

12 나는 달이 지구 주위를 돈다는 것을 안다. (go)

→ I know that the moon ___________ around the Earth.

C 다음 두 문장의 의미가 같도록 빈칸에 알맞은 말을 쓰시오.

1 Emily said, "I am tired."

= Emily said that she ___________ tired.

2 He said, "I can write a letter."

= He said that he ___________ write a letter.

3 They said, "We must go to school."

= They said that ___________ had to go to school.

4 Emma said, "I am happy now."

= Emma said that she was happy ___________ ___________ ___________.

5 Jack said, "I will visit my uncle."

= Jack said that ___________ would visit ___________ uncle.

6 Sam said, "I will go to the zoo tomorrow."

= Sam said that he would go to the zoo ___________ ___________ ___________.

7 Ben said, "I saw a bird yesterday."

= Ben said that he ___________ ___________ a bird the day before.

8 David said, "I must finish my homework today."

= David said that he had to finish his homework ___________ ___________.

9 Olivia said that she had a cat.

= Olivia said, "___________ ___________ a cat."

10 Anna said that she could run fast.

= Anna said, "I ___________ ___________ fast."

11 Lucy said that she could swim well.

= Lucy said, "___________ ___________ swim well."

12 Tom said that he would do his homework.

= Tom said, "___________ ___________ do my homework."

D 다음 문장의 밑줄 친 부분을 어법상 바르게 고치시오.

1 She asked where <u>did I go</u>.

→ _______________________________________

2 He told me <u>clean</u> my room.

→ _______________________________________

3 They asked me if <u>do I like</u> cake.

→ _______________________________________

4 I asked why <u>was he</u> crying.

→ _______________________________________

5 He <u>said</u> me to open the door.

→ _______________________________________

6 She asked where <u>is the cat</u>.

→ _______________________________________

7 Mom told me <u>that close</u> the window.

→ _______________________________________

8 I ask <u>will she come</u> early.

→ _______________________________________

9 He said <u>me</u>, "Don't run."

→ _______________________________________

10 Do you know <u>what means this word</u>?

→ _______________________________________

11 Let me know <u>when will the concert start</u>.

→ _______________________________________

12 I don't know <u>how long will they stay</u>.

→ _______________________________________

13 Can you tell me <u>where is my umbrella</u>?

→ _______________________________________

14 I wonder <u>what did he say</u> to you.

→ _______________________________________

15 Do you know <u>how tall is she</u>?

→ _______________________________________

A 다음 문장에서 어법상 틀린 곳을 찾아 바르게 고치시오.

1 Half of the members is missing.

_______________ → _______________

2 Lots of rice come from Asia.

_______________ → _______________

3 A lot of cars passes this road.

_______________ → _______________

4 That he passed all the tests are true.

_______________ → _______________

5 Nothing make him smile these days.

_______________ → _______________

6 Either you or your friends is invited.

_______________ → _______________

7 Swimming every day keep her strong.

_______________ → _______________

8 Whether he comes or not don't matter.

_______________ → _______________

9 Something smell strange in the kitchen.

_______________ → _______________

10 Plenty of information are available online.

_______________ → _______________

11 A number of players who are tall is in the team.

_______________ → _______________

12 One of the cakes that look delicious are chocolate.

_______________ → _______________

13 Each of the answers that seem wrong are correct.

_______________ → _______________

14 Both the teacher and the students agrees on the rule.

_______________ → _______________

15 My phone as well as my keys are in the bag.

_______________ → _______________

1 그는 서울로 이사하기 전에 거기에 갔었다고 말했다.

→ He said that he ___________ ___________ there before he moved to Seoul.

2 나는 그가 내일 떠날 것이라는 것을 믿는다.

→ I believe that he ___________ ___________ tomorrow.

3 그녀는 늦게 도착했다고 말했다.

→ She said that she ___________ ___________ late.

4 그는 그가 그 책을 이미 읽었다고 말했다.

→ He said that he ___________ ___________ the book already.

5 나는 그가 지금 밖에 있다고 생각한다.

→ I think that he ___________ outside now.

6 그는 새로운 컴퓨터를 샀다고 말했다.

→ He said that he ___________ ___________ a new computer.

7 나는 네가 착한 학생이라는 것을 안다.

→ I know that you ___________ a good student.

8 그녀는 어제 아프다고 말했다.

→ She said that she ___________ sick yesterday.

9 그는 그것을 잊어버렸다고 말했다.

→ He said that he ___________ ___________ it.

10 나는 그녀가 피아노를 잘 치는 것을 안다.

→ I know that she ___________ the piano well.

11 나는 그가 매일 아침에 뛰는 것을 안다.

→ I know that he ___________ every morning.

12 그는 늦게 잠자리에 들었다고 말했다.

→ He said that he ___________ ___________ to bed late.

C 다음 문장을 간접화법으로 바꿔 쓰시오.

1 James said, "I'm busy."

→ _______________________________________

2 Emma said, "I have to go home."

→ _______________________________________

3 Mia said, "I have a new phone."

→ _______________________________________

4 Tom said, "I can play the guitar."

→ _______________________________________

5 Ben said, "I will go to the library."

→ _______________________________________

6 Mike said, "I'm going to school."

→ _______________________________________

7 Jack said, "I'm playing soccer."

→ _______________________________________

8 Lucy said, "I'm sleepy now."

→ _______________________________________

9 Olivia said, "I can finish it today."

→ _______________________________________

10 Henry said, "I will see her tomorrow."

→ _______________________________________

11 Daniel said, "I finished my lunch."

→ _______________________________________

12 Minho said, "I watched TV yesterday."

→ _______________________________________

D 다음 우리말에 맞도록 괄호 안의 단어들을 바르게 배열하시오.

1 그는 내가 어디로 가고 있는지 물었다.
(asked / he / going / where / was / I / .)

→ _______________________________________

2 그녀는 누가 문을 닫았는지 물었다.
(asked / the / who / she / door / closed / .)

→ _______________________________________

3 그는 내가 언제 도착했었는지 물었다.
(asked / had / arrived / he / I / when / .)

→ _______________________________________

4 그녀는 내가 그 가방을 들어줄 수 있는지 물었다.
(the / if / asked / she / carry / could / bag / I / .)

→ _______________________________________

5 너는 그가 어디에 있는지 아니?
(where / is / he / know / do / you / ?)

→ _______________________________________

6 너는 내가 언제 일어나는지 아니?
(do / when / up / get / know / you / I / ?)

→ _______________________________________

7 그녀가 키가 얼마나 큰지 말해 줄 수 있니?
(you / me / tall / tell / how / she / can / is / ?)

→ _______________________________________

8 너는 그녀가 왜 화가 났는지 아니?
(know / why / angry / you / is / do / she / ?)

→ _______________________________________

9 나는 이 앱이 어떻게 작동하는지 궁금하다.
(this / how / app / wonder / I / works / .)

→ _______________________________________

10 너는 그 식당이 어디에 있는지 아니?
(the restaurant / do / know / is / where / you / ?)

→ _______________________________________

[1–2] 다음 중 빈칸에 들어갈 말로 가장 적절한 것을 고르시오.

1

> A number of students _________ late today.

① is

② are

③ was

④ being

⑤ has been

2

> I didn't know why she _________ so angry.

① is

② are

③ was

④ will be

⑤ were

[3–4] 다음 중 어법상 옳은 것을 고르시오.

3

① He said he is happy.

② He said he was happy.

③ He said he be happy.

④ He said he will happy.

⑤ He said he has be happy.

4

① He said that he is hungry.

② She told me she will be late.

③ I thought she knows the answer.

④ They believed the story was true.

⑤ We learned that the sun rose in the east.

[5–6] 다음 문장을 영어로 바르게 옮긴 것은?

5

> 나는 그가 어디에 사는지 궁금하다.

① I wonder where he lives.

② I wonder where is he living.

③ I wonder where does he live.

④ I wondered where did he live.

⑤ I am wondering where does he live.

6

> 그는 내가 언제 도착했는지 물었다.

① He asks when I arrive.

② He said when I arrived.

③ He wonder when I arrive.

④ He asked when did I arrive.

⑤ He asked when I had arrived.

[7-8] 빈칸에 알맞은 말을 써서 다음 문장을 간접화법으로 바꾸시오.

7

He said, "Did you finish your homework?"

→ He asked me ___________________ ___________ my homework.

8

"Be careful!" the teacher said.

→ The teacher told us _______________ careful.

9 다음 대화의 빈칸에 들어갈 말이 바르게 짝지어진 것은?

A: Did you talk to Ms. Lee this morning?
B: Yes, she ______ me why I ______ absent yesterday.

① asks – am

② asks – was

③ asked – was

④ asked – am

⑤ has asked - has been

[10-11] 다음 우리말에 맞도록 빈칸에 알맞은 말을 쓰시오.

10

내 반 친구들 중 한 명이 기타를 연주한다.

→ _______________ of my classmates _______________ the guitar.

11

David는 그녀가 어디에 사는지 물어보았다.

→ David asked ______________ _______________ _______________.

[12-13] 다음 중 어법상 **틀린** 것을 고르시오.

12

① Everything is ready.

② A lot of time was wasted.

③ There have been a mistake.

④ Half of the apples are red.

⑤ The old remember the war.

13

① He told me not to open the door.

② He said that he had been to the library.

③ She asked me if I liked music.

④ I really wonder what does he want.

⑤ A group of students are going on a trip.

[14-15] 다음 문장에서 어법상 **틀린** 곳을 찾아 바르게 고치시오.

14

The number of students who need help are increasing.

________________ → ________________

15

All of the pens that she bought was cheap.

________________ → ________________

[16-17] 다음 우리말에 맞도록 괄호 안의 단어들을 바르게 배열하시오.

16 

그가 어디 있는지 내게 말해.
(he / tell / where / me / is / .)

→ ________________________________

17

나는 그가 어떻게 영어를 말하는 것을 배우게 되었는지 궁금하다.
(how / learned / to speak / he / I / wonder / English / .)

→ ________________________________

[18-19] 다음 문장을 간접화법으로 바르게 바꾼 것을 고르시오.

18

Lucy said, "I will call you tonight."

① Lucy said that she will call you tonight.

② Lucy said that she would call me that night.

③ Lucy said that she called you that night.

④ Lucy said that I would call her tonight.

⑤ Lucy said that she would call you that night.

Mark said, "I will meet you here tomorrow."

① Mark said that he will meet me here tomorrow.
② Mark said that he would meet me there the next day.
③ Mark said that I would meet him here the next day.
④ Mark said that he will met me there tomorrow.
⑤ Mark said that he would meet you there the next day.

[20–21] 다음 대화에서 어법상 <u>틀린</u> 곳을 찾아 바르게 고치시오.

20

A: Did Tom call you?
B: Yes, he said that he will visit me the next day.

_________________ → _________________

21

A: Both my brother and my sister lives in Seoul.
B: Oh, do they meet often?
A: No, each of them are very busy with work.

_________________ → _________________

_________________ → _________________

22 다음 중 어법상 옳은 것을 <u>모두</u> 고르면?

① They told me that they get a new car.
② He said that he had never heard that song.
③ Not the students but the teacher were angry.
④ Everything that happens in these stories is true.
⑤ To travel many countries require courage.

23 다음 글의 밑줄 친 부분 중 어법상 옳은 것끼리 바르게 짝지어진 것은?

Jane and Daniel were going to meet at the café at 3 p.m. It was already almost four but Daniel didn't come yet. She wondered if he ⓐhad missed the bus or if something ⓑhad happened. She didn't know why he ⓒwill be late. After waiting for another ten minutes, she finally ⓓsaw Daniel rushing toward the café, out of breath. He apologized and explained that the bus ⓔbreaks down.

① ⓐ, ⓑ
② ⓐ, ⓑ, ⓒ
③ ⓐ, ⓑ, ⓓ
④ ⓑ, ⓒ, ⓔ
⑤ ⓑ, ⓒ, ⓓ

비교

- 비교 표현의 개념과 형태
- 원급 비교 as~as 용법
- 비교급
- 최상급

비교 표현의 개념과 형태

구문		원급	비교급	최상급
대부분의 형용사/부사	-er, -est	fast / old(나이 든)	fast**er** / old**er**	fast**est** / old**est**
-e로 끝나는 경우	-r, -st	nice	nic**er**	nic**est**
모음+자음	끝자음 한 번 더	big	big**ger**	big**gest**
-y로 끝나는 경우	y → i 변경	happy	happ**ier**	happ**iest**
-ful, less, ous / 3음절 이상	more / most	beautiful interesting	**more** beautiful **more** interesting	**most** beautiful **most** interesting
-ly로 끝나는 경우	more / most	quickly	**more** quickly	**most** quickly
불규칙 변화		good / well	better	best
		bad / badly	worse	worst
		many / much	more	most
		little	less	least
		far	farther / further	farthest / furthest
		old(손위의)	elder	eldest

A 다음 중 올바른 비교급 또는 최상급에 ○를 표시하시오.

1 fast

faster ( )

more fast ( )

2 nice

most nice ( )

nicest ( )

3 happy

happyer ( )

happier ( )

4 many

most ( )

maniest ( )

원급 비교 as~as 용법

~만큼 ~한(하게)	A as + 형용사/부사의 원급 + as B A는 B만큼 ~하다 (→ A와 B가 비슷함) He is as tall as his father. (He = father)	
~만큼 ~하지 않은(않게)	A not as[so] + 형용사/부사의 원급 + as B A는 B만큼 ~하지 않다 (→ B가 더 ~하다) He is not as tall as his father. (He < father)	as big as

- as + 형용사/부사의 원급 + as possible: 가능한 한 ~한(하게)
  He runs **as** fast **as possible**. = He runs as fast as he can.
- 배수사 + as + 형용사/부사의 원급 + as : ~보다 몇 배만큼 ~한(하게)
  This tree is **twice as** tall **as** that one. (이 나무는 저 나무보다 두 배나 높다.)

B 다음 괄호 안에서 알맞은 것을 고르시오.

1 He is as (big / bigger) as I am.

2 He swam as (fast / fastest) as possible.

3 This pencil is not as (long / longer) as that one.

A 형용사/부사의 비교급 + than B
A는 B보다 더 ~하다

A watermelon is bigger than an apple.
Shane is taller than Mike.
She is more popular than her sister.

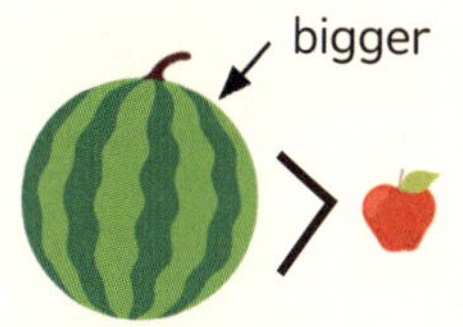

- 비교급 앞에 much, even, far, a lot을 붙여 '훨씬'이라는 뜻으로 비교급을 강조함.
  This yellow car is **much bigger** than the red one.
- the + 비교급, the + 비교급: ~하면 할수록 더 ~하다.
  The earlier you start, **the sooner** you can finish.
- 비교급 + and + 비교급: 점점 더 ~한(하게)
  It's getting **colder and colder**.

C 다음 괄호 안에서 알맞은 것을 고르시오.

1   My room is (clean / cleaner) than yours.

2   He runs faster (as / than) his brother.

3   The more you practice, (easier / the easier) it becomes.

the + 형용사/부사의 최상급
가장 ~한(하게)

She studies the hardest in her class.
She is the kindest person I have ever met.

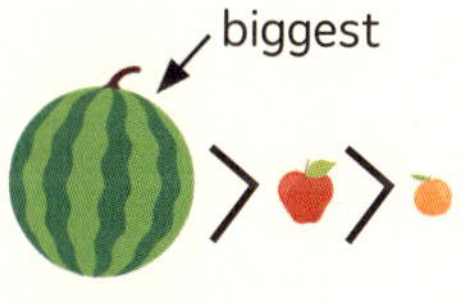

- 최상급 앞에 the를 사용하지 않는 경우
  - 소유격이 앞에 오는 경우 : He is my best friend. / She is his closest relative.
  - 부사 최상급인 경우 the 생략 가능
  He runs (the) **fastest** in class. (runs 수식)
  Who can jump (the) **highest**? (jump 수식)

D 다음 중 어법상 옳은 문장에 ○를 표시하시오.

1   She is the most tallest student in the class.   (   )

    She is the tallest student in the class.   (   )

2   This is best cake I have ever eaten.   (   )

    This is the best cake I have ever eaten.   (   )

A 다음 중 비교급과 최상급의 형태가 옳으면 ○, 틀리면 X를 표시하시오.

1   small - smaller - smallest   (   )

2   young - younger - youngest   (   )

3   long - longger - longest   (   )

4   warm - warmer - warmest   (   )

5   big - bigger - biggest   (   )

6   hot - hotter - hottest   (   )

7   thin - thiner - thinest   (   )

8   late - later - latest   (   )

9   old - oldder - olddest   (   )

10   wise - wiser - wisest   (   )

11   easy - easier - easiest   (   )

12   busy - busyer - busyest   (   )

13   funny - funnier - funniest   (   )

14   beautiful - more beautiful - most beautiful   (   )

15   expensive - expensiver - expensivest   (   )

B 다음 그림에 맞도록 빈칸에 알맞은 말을 쓰시오.

1. tall	2. tall	3. big	4. fast	5. tall
Minsu James	Mia Kim		Clark Martin	that this

1   Minsu is ___________ ___________ ___________ James.

2   ___________ is not as tall as ___________.

3   The apple is ___________ ___________ ___________ the orange.

4   Clark does ___________ run ___________ ___________ as Martin.

5   This tree is ___________ ___________ ___________ as that one.

 다음 괄호 안에서 알맞은 것을 고르시오.

1 He runs (fast / faster) than me.

2 My bike is (cheap / cheaper) than his.

3 She is (young / younger) than her sister.

4 Today is as (cold / colder) as yesterday.

5 This street is as (wide / wider) as that one.

6 This box is (heavy / heavier) than that one.

7 The movie was as (interesting / more interesting) as the book.

8 This chair is as (comfortable / more comfortable) as the other one.

9 She is the (older / eldest) daughter in the family.

10 The KTX is the (quickest / most quick) way to travel across the country.

D 다음 표의 정보와 괄호 안의 단어를 이용하여 빈칸에 알맞은 단어를 쓰시오. (단, 필요시 어형을 바꿀 것)

Name	Study Hours	Bike Riding Speed (km/h)	Cellphone Use
Lisa	3 hours	15	1 hour
Emma	5 hours	12	3 hours
Noah	4 hours	18	2 hours

1 Emma studies ____________ than Lisa every day. (long)

2 Noah doesn't study as ____________ as Emma. (much)

3 Emma rides her bike ____________ ____________ than the other two. (slow)

4 Noah is the ____________ cyclist among them. (fast)

5 Lisa uses her phone the ____________ each day. (less)

6 Noah uses his phone ____________ than Emma. (little)

A 다음 중 단어의 알맞은 비교급과 최상급을 빈칸에 쓰시오.

1 kind - ____________________ - ____________________

2 large - ____________________ - ____________________

3 close - ____________________ - ____________________

4 fat - ____________________ - ____________________

5 sad - ____________________ - ____________________

6 lucky - ____________________ - ____________________

7 pretty - ____________________ - ____________________

8 early - ____________________ - ____________________

9 good - ____________________ - ____________________

10 bad - ____________________ - ____________________

11 much - ____________________ - ____________________

12 little - ____________________ - ____________________

13 far - ____________________ - ____________________

14 clever - ____________________ - ____________________

15 narrow - ____________________ - ____________________

16 simple - ____________________ - ____________________

17 bright - ____________________ - ____________________

18 low - ____________________ - ____________________

19 famous - ____________________ - ____________________

20 comfortable - ____________________ - ____________________

1   My bag is as heavy than yours. ( )

2   Today is as colder as yesterday. ( )

3   My house is as big as my uncle's. ( )

4   Please drive as slowly as possible. ( )

5   Try to write as neatly as possible. ( )

6   We must speak as clear as possible. ( )

7   My cat is not as playful as my dog. ( )

8   The soup is not as salt as yesterday. ( )

9   This road is as long as the other one. ( )

10 This pizza is as delicious to the pasta. ( )

11 This book is as interesting as that one. ( )

12 The movie was as funny as the cartoon. ( )

13 The giraffe is three times as tall as the zebra. ( )

14 The park is twice as large as the playground. ( )

15 This chair is not so comfortable as the sofa. ( )

16 She ran as fast as possible to catch the bus. ( )

17 This street is not as noisier as the main road. ( )

18 The train is three times as fast than the bus. ( )

19 My handwriting is not as clear than my sister's. ( )

20 The new book is twice as thick as the old book. ( )

C 다음 괄호 안에서 알맞은 것을 고르시오.

1 My brother is as (tall / taller) as me.

2 The train is (fast / faster) than the car.

3 Today is (sunny / sunnier) than yesterday.

4 The river is as (wide / wider) as the road.

5 The hill is longer (as / than) I thought.

6 My backpack is lighter (as / than) yours.

7 The park is as clean (as / than) the garden.

8 Her voice is softer (as / than) her sister's.

9 The team played as well (as / than) possible.

10 My handwriting is neater (as / than) before.

11 His explanation is (clear / clearer) than mine.

12 My bike is as (new / newer) as my friend's bike.

13 This puzzle is (easy / easier) than the last one.

14 This street is (narrow / narrower) than that one.

15 This jacket is (as warm / warmer) than the blue one.

16 I will answer as (honestly / more honestly) as possible.

17 Your drawing is as (beautiful / more beautiful) as hers.

18 This store is as (crowded / more crowded) as the market.

19 The fish is twice as (big as / bigger than) the one I caught.

20 This computer is (cheap / cheaper) than the one in the shop.

D 다음 중 괄호 안의 단어를 이용하여 빈칸에 알맞은 형태로 쓰시오.

1   His room is _____________ than mine. (messy)

2   This box is _____________ than that one. (big)

3   This is the _____________ blanket I own. (soft)

4   This is the _____________ tree in the park. (old)

5   Please run as _____________ as possible. (slowly)

6   She is the _____________ _____________ friend I have. (honest)

7   She is the _____________ girl in the class. (happy)

8   That was the _____________ storm in decades. (big)

9   His shoes are as _____________ as mine. (expensive)

10 She is the _____________ cook in the kitchen. (great)

11 The cake is _____________ than the cookies. (sweet)

12 This is the _____________ _____________ park in the city. (peaceful)

13 He is the _____________ actor in the movie. (funny)

14 This street is _____________ than the main road. (quiet)

15 That was the _____________ bridge I've ever crossed. (long)

16 We should save water as _____________ as possible. (much)

17 She is the _____________ _____________ neighbor in the town. (generous)

18 This movie is the _____________ _____________ I have ever seen. (interesting)

19 The river here is _____________ than the one in the city. (clean)

20 The coffee here tastes _____________ than the one at the other café. (good)

A 다음 우리말에 맞도록 괄호 안의 단어를 알맞은 형태로 바꿔 쓰시오.

1 우리 교실은 도서관만큼 밝다. (bright)

→ Our classroom is _________________________ the library.

2 이 케이크는 사탕만큼 달다. (sweet)

→ This cake is _________________________ the candy.

3 그 언덕은 그 산만큼 높다. (high)

→ The hill is _________________________ the mountain.

4 그 음악은 드럼 소리만큼 크다. (loud)

→ The music is _________________________ the sound of the drum.

5 그녀의 눈은 하늘만큼 파랗다. (blue)

→ Her eyes are _________________________ the sky.

6 내 연필은 네 것만큼 길다. (long)

→ My pencil is _________________________ yours.

7 이 문제는 지난 문제만큼 쉽다. (easy)

→ This question is _________________________ the last one.

8 내 휴대폰은 펜만큼 가볍다. (light)

→ My phone is _________________________ a pen.

9 내 남동생은 아버지만큼 힘이 세다. (strong)

→ My brother is _________________________ my father.

10 그는 가능한 한 크게 노래했다. (loudly)

→ He sang _________________________.

11 그녀는 가능한 한 멀리 수영했다. (far)

→ She swam _________________________.

12 나는 가능한 한 많이 읽을 것이다. (much)

→ I will read _________________________.

1 내 컴퓨터는 네 것만큼 빠르지 않다. (fast)
→ My computer is _______________________ yours.

2 이 강은 그 호수만큼 깊지 않다. (deep)
→ This river is _______________________ the lake.

3 그 케이크는 빵만큼 신선하지 않다. (fresh)
→ The cake is _______________________ the bread.

4 내 배낭은 Tom의 것만큼 무겁지 않다. (heavy)
→ My backpack is _______________________ Tom's.

5 내 차는 그의 차보다 두 배 빠르다. (fast)
→ My car is _______________________ his car.

6 그녀의 머리카락은 내 것보다 세 배 길다. (long)
→ Her hair is _______________________ mine.

7 그녀의 미소는 태양보다 더 밝다. (bright)
→ Her smile is _______________________ the sun.

8 이 도로는 지름길보다 더 안전하다. (safe)
→ This road is _______________________ the shortcut.

9 이 과일은 저것보다 더 즙이 많다. (juicy)
→ This fruit is _______________________ that one.

10 그의 농담은 네 것보다 더 재미있다. (funny)
→ His jokes are _______________________ yours.

11 그 버스는 평소보다 더 붐빈다. (crowded)
→ The bus is _______________________ usual.

12 내 개는 이웃집 개보다 더 다정하다. (friendly)
→ My dog is _______________________ my neighbor's dog.

C 다음 괄호 안의 단어들을 바르게 배열하시오.

1 (possible / high / jumped / as / as / he / .)

→ ____

2 (as / yours / not / my glass / full / is / as / .)

→ ____

3 (the trees / taller / than / is / the tower / .)

→ ____

4 (before / the road / than / smoother / is / .)

→ ____

5 (than / these shoes / expensive / the old jacket / are / more / .)

→ ____

6 (as / the old coins / valuable / are / as / gold / .)

→ ____

7 (my pants / than / cleaner / my shirt / is / .)

→ ____

8 (week / than / last / cooler / is / the weather / .)

→ ____

9 (average / than / were / better / her scores / .)

→ ____

10 (yesterday / stronger / are / than / the waves / .)

→ ____

11 (the photos / not / vivid / is / as / the painting / as / .)

→ ____

12 (exciting / more / golf / than / are / team sports / .)

→ ____

D 다음 대화의 괄호 안에서 알맞은 것을 고르시오.

1 A: Is my desk (wide / wider) than his?

   B: No, his desk is three times (wider / as wide) as yours.

2 A: Is my bag (heavy / heavier) than Tom's?

   B: No, Tom's bag is twice (heavier / as heavy) as yours.

3 A: Is your car (fast / faster) than mine?

   B: Yes, it's (much / very) faster than yours.

4 A: Is this river (deep / deeper) than the lake?

   B: No, the lake is three times (deeper/ as deep) as the river.

5 A: Is this shirt as (cheap / cheaper) as the blue one?

   B: No, it's (even / very) cheaper than that one.

6 A: Was Mark's joke as (funny / funnier) as mine?

   B: No, that was the (funny / funniest) joke I've ever heard.

7 A: Was the test as (easy / easier) as you thought?

   B: Actually, it was the (easy / easiest) test I've had all year.

8 A: Was the movie as (exciting / more exciting) as the book?

   B: Yes, it was the (more exciting / most exciting) film I've ever seen.

9 A: Was her speech as (inspiring / more inspiring) as last year's?

   B: It was the (inspiring / most inspiring) speech I've heard in years.

10 A: Was your trip as (memorable / more memorable) as last summer's?

   B: Yes, it was the (more memorable / most memorable) holiday of my life.

1 다음 중 비교급 형태가 <u>틀린</u> 것은?

① bigger

② more interesting

③ more happier

④ farther

⑤ better

2 다음 중 최상급 형태가 <u>틀린</u> 것은?

① most comfortable

② most delicious

③ most funny

④ lightest

⑤ worst

3 다음 중 어법상 옳은 것은?

① She is as taller as her sister.

② The test is as easier as last time.

③ This street is as safer as that one.

④ Today is not so colder as yesterday.

⑤ This book is not as interesting as that one.

4 다음 빈칸에 들어갈 말로 가장 적절한 것은?

This box is _________ than it looks.

① heavy   ② heaviest

③ heavier   ④ more heavy

⑤ most heavy

5 다음 빈칸에 들어갈 말로 적절하지 <u>않은</u> 것은?

This road is _________ longer than the old one.

① much   ② a lot

③ even   ④ very

⑤ far

6 다음 문장이 의미하는 것은?

The classroom is not as warm as the library.

① The library is as warm as the school.

② The classroom is warmer than the library.

③ The library is warmer than the classroom.

④ The library is not warmer than the classroom.

⑤ The classroom is the warmest room in the school.

다음 대화의 빈칸에 공통으로 들어갈 말로 가장 적절한 것은?

A: Was the river as clean ______ the lake?
B: No, it was not so clean ______ the lake.

① so
② as
③ for
④ than
⑤ to

8 다음 중 빈칸에 들어갈 말이 바르게 짝지어진 것은?

- The more you smile, the ______ you feel.
- This is the ______ summer in ten years.

① happy - hot
② happier - hottest
③ happier - hotter
④ happiest - hottest
⑤ happiest - hotter

[9-11] 다음 우리말에 맞도록 빈칸에 알맞은 말을 쓰시오.

9

그 의사는 가능한 한 빠르게 왔다.

→ The doctor came ___________ soon ___________ ___________.

10

이 책은 사전만큼 두껍지는 않다.

→ The book is ___________ ___________ thick ___________ the dictionary.

11

그의 배낭은 내 것보다 세 배 더 무겁다.

→ His backpack is three ___________ ___________ heavy ___________ mine.

[12-14] 다음 그림에 맞도록 괄호 안의 단어들을 이용하여 빈칸에 알맞은 문장을 쓰시오.(단, 필요시 어형을 바꿀 것)

12

(not, is, as, tall)

→ ___________________________________

13

(the rabbit, much, than, the pig, small)

→ _______________________________

14

(short, the, Vivian, girl)

→ _______________________________

15 다음 중 어법상 <u>틀린</u> 것을 고르시오.

① They completed the task faster than expected.

② We arrived much earlier than we had planned.

③ He speaks English the most fluently in our class.

④ I read books more often than I watch movies.

⑤ She sings as beautiful as a professional singer.

16 다음 중 어법상 <u>틀린</u> 문장을 모두 고르면?

① I play the piano as well as my sister.

② She studies much harder than before.

③ He runs the most fastest in the school.

④ The party last night was most enjoyable.

⑤ They drive not as carefully as their parents.

[17-18] 다음 문장에서 어법상 <u>틀린</u> 곳을 찾아 바르게 고치시오.

17

She tried to solve the problem as easy as possible.

_______________ → _______________

18

The shop is twice as bigger as the one next to it.

_______________ → _______________

[19-20] **다음 우리말에 맞도록 괄호 안의 단어들을 바르게 배열하여 문장을 완성하시오.**

19

나는 읽으면 읽을수록 이해가 깊어진다.
(understand / more / I / the)

→ The more I read, ___________________

___________________.

20

사람들은 현금을 점점 덜 사용하고 있다.
(are / cash / less / and / using / less)

→ People ___________________

___________________.

21 다음 대화의 빈칸에 들어갈 말이 바르게 짝지어진 것은?

A: Who helped you with your project?
B: Sarah. She is the __________ person I know.
A: Oh, I've heard she's always willing to help others.
B: Yes, she's as __________ as a teacher when explaining things.

① kind - patiently

② kinder - patient

③ kindest - patiently

④ kindest - patient

⑤ kindest - more patient

22 다음 중 표의 내용과 일치하는 문장을 <u>모두</u> 고르면?

Name	Height (cm)	Running Speed (km/h)	Age
Alex	165	12	14
Brian	170	10	15
Chris	160	14	13

① Alex is taller than Chris.

② Brian runs faster than Alex.

③ Chris is the youngest among them.

④ Brian is as tall as Chris.

⑤ Chris runs the fastest of the three.

23 다음 글의 밑줄 친 부분 중 어법상 옳은 것끼리 바르게 짝지어진 것은?

Last Friday, we went to a new Italian restaurant in town. The place was ⓐ<u>cozier</u> than the one we visited before. I ordered a pizza with cheese and mushrooms, while my friend chose one with pepperoni. When the food arrived, I took a bite and ⓑ<u>smiled</u>. "This pizza is as ⓒ<u>delicious</u> ⓓ<u>than</u> the one we had last week," I said. My friend nodded. "And their garlic bread is the ⓔ<u>better</u> I've ever eaten," she said.

① ⓐ, ⓑ, ⓔ

② ⓐ, ⓑ, ⓒ

③ ⓐ, ⓒ, ⓓ

④ ⓑ, ⓒ, ⓔ

⑤ ⓒ, ⓓ, ⓔ

8

특수 구문

- 강조
- 의미상의 주어
- 병렬
- 도치

강조

1. do / does / did + 동사원형: '정말로', '확실히'			
주어	시제	규칙	예문
I / You / We / They	현재	do + 동사원형	I do like this song.
He / She / It	현재	does + 동사원형	He does know the answer.
모든 주어	과거	did + 동사원형	He did finish his homework.

2. It is / was + 강조 대상 + that + 나머지 문장	
강조 대상	예문
주어	It was Tom that[who] opened the door.
목적어	It was a new bag that[which] she bought.
부사(구)	It was yesterday that[when] she called me.
부사(구)	It was in the park that[where] I met him.

A 다음 괄호 안에서 알맞은 것을 고르시오.

1 They (did / are) visit Paris last summer.

2 He (do / does) remember your birthday.

3 It was my teacher (that / which) encouraged me.

의미상의 주어

to부정사나 동명사의 동작을 실제로 하는 주체		
종류	형태	예문
to부정사의 의미상의 주어	for + 목적격 (일반적) of + 목적격 (사람의 성격이나 성질)	It is important for you to sleep early. It was kind of her to help me.
동명사의 의미상의 주어	소유격 또는 목적격	I don't like his singing loudly. We enjoyed them playing soccer.

B 다음 문장에서 의미상의 주어를 찾아 밑줄 치시오.

1 It is important for you to study hard.

2 It was rude of Sam to speak like that.

3 I heard about Sujin's joining the soccer team.

접속사로 연결되는 단어나 구, 절의 문법적 형태를 서로 일치시키는 것	
형태	예문
단어	They sang, danced, and laughed all night. (동사) The movie was not only funny but also touching. (형용사)
구 / 절	She is interested in music but not in sports. (전치사구) He enjoys neither reading novels nor watching TV. (동명사구) He ran quickly, and he caught the bus. (절)

C 다음 괄호 안에서 알맞은 것을 고르시오.

1 She is both kind and (intelligent / intelligence).

2 He likes reading books and (play / playing) soccer.

3 She spends time playing the piano and (practicing / to practice) singing.

도치

정상적인 어순(주어 + 동사)을 바꾸어, 동사가 주어보다 먼저 나오게 하는 것	
형태	예문
장소 부사(구) 도치	At the corner was a small café. Into the room came the teacher.
부정어(구) 도치 (Never, little, hardly, rarely, no, not, not only 등)	Never is she late for school. 「부정어 + be동사 + 주어」 Hardly can I believe this story. 「부정어 + 조동사 + 주어 + 동사원형」 Rarely do they play outside. 「부정어 + do/does/did + 주어 + 동사원형」
So / Neither 도치	긍정문 뒤: 「so + 동사 + 주어」 (~도 역시 그러하다) I am happy. / So am I. He can sing well. / So can I.
	부정문 뒤: 「neither + 동사 + 주어」 (~도 역시 그렇지 않다) I am not hungry. / Neither am I. He doesn't like math. / Neither does she.

D 다음 괄호 안에서 강조 표현을 고르시오.

1 Under the tree (sat two children / two children sat).

2 Never (the town was / was the town) so peaceful.

3 I don't live in Seoul, and neither (do / does) my cousin.

A 다음 괄호 안에서 알맞은 강조 표현을 고르시오.

1 I (do / will) like this idea a lot.

2 She (do / did) finish the project before the deadline.

3 He (does / can) look very tired today.

4 We (do / will) believe your story.

5 We (are / did) hear a strange noise outside.

6 My friend (do / does) look happy today.

7 They (do / does) like playing basketball after school.

8 Mina (do / does) want to join the club.

B 다음 문장에서 강조하는 대상을 찾아 밑줄 치시오.

1 It is Tom that won the prize.

2 It was my friend who helped me.

3 It is this book that I want.

4 It was her voice that surprised me.

5 It is at school that we meet.

6 It is on the beach that we take a walk in summer.

7 It is today that we start the project.

C 다음 문장에서 의미상의 주어를 찾아 밑줄 치시오.

1 It was difficult for him to carry the heavy box.

2 It was kind of her to share her lunch.

3 We were surprised at their winning the game.

4 It was wise of him to save money regularly.

5 It was foolish of her to believe that story.

보기   see   sees   saw   seen   seeing

1 그는 여러 곳을 여행했고 많은 사람을 보았다.

→ He has traveled many places and ___________ many people.

2 그녀는 새로운 사람들을 만나고 오래된 친구들을 본다.

→ She meets new people and ___________ her old friends.

3 나는 새소리를 듣고 나무를 볼 수 있다.

→ I can hear the birds and ___________ the trees.

4 우리는 박물관을 방문했고 그림들을 보았다.

→ We visited the museum and ___________ the paintings.

5 그녀는 늦게까지 일하는 것과 일몰을 보는 것에 익숙하다.

→ She is used to working late and ___________ the sunset.

E 다음 문장의 밑줄 친 부분을 어법상 바르게 고치시오.

1 Beside the river <u>the fishing boat was</u>.   → _______________

2 Never <u>the room was</u> so quiet.   → _______________

3 Hardly <u>they will forget</u> such a wonderful trip.   → _______________

4 Little <u>they know</u> about my plan.   → _______________

5 She is a good singer, and so <u>her sister is</u>.   → _______________

6 He didn't understand the question, and neither <u>I did</u>. → _______________

7 Behind the curtain <u>the singer stood</u>.   → _______________

8 Never <u>I have seen</u> such a beautiful sunrise.   → _______________

9 Seldom <u>he complains</u> about his work.   → _______________

10 I'm not going to the party, neither <u>she is</u>.   → _______________

A 다음 중 강조 문장이 되도록 괄호 안에서 알맞은 것을 고르시오.

1   You (do / should) speak English very fluently.

2   I (do / does) enjoy listening to classical music.

3   You (did / might) remember to bring your homework.

4   I (am / do) feel nervous before a big test.

5   You (are / do) know a lot about computers.

6   My teacher (do / does) explain things very clearly.

7   We (does / did) hear a strange story from him.

8   My friend (do / does) seem very confident today.

9   She (do / does) pay attention in every class.

10   My mom (does / will) enjoy shopping at that store.

11   They (do / does) love visiting new places every summer.

12   My dad (does / can) cook delicious food at home.

13   He (do / does) practice basketball every afternoon.

14   They (are / did) win the game last week.

15   I do (like / liked) spicy food very much.

16   She does (enjoy / enjoys) watching dramas at night.

17   We did (hear / heard) a loud sound.

18   I did (see / saw) him at the library yesterday.

19   We do (need / needed) more information before we decide.

20   He did (make / makes) a good impression on the teacher.

1   It was my mother (which / that) raised me.

2   It is my father (who / which) cooks dinner every Sunday.

3   It is this painting (who / that) attracts many visitors to the museum.

4   It will be next week (when / where) we take the exam.

5   It was Sarah (who / which) called me last night.

6   It was this movie (which / what) won the award.

7   It was his smile (who / which) made me happy.

8   It will be next month (when / where) we travel to Paris.

9   It is the science lab (when / that) students do their experiments.

10 It will be the new stadium (when / that) the final match takes place.

C 다음 괄호 안에서 알맞은 것을 고르시오.

1   It is important (to you / for you) to get enough sleep.

2   It was careless (of him / to him) to forget the meeting.

3   It is necessary for (we / us) to finish the homework today.

4   It was kind (of her / for her) to help the old man.

5   It was wise of (them / they) to save some money.

6   It is natural (to children / for children) to make mistakes.

7   Everyone enjoyed (your / yours) dancing at the festival.

8   I appreciate (he / him) helping me yesterday.

9   I was proud of (her / she) passing the driving test.

10 My parents won't mind (I / me) staying out late.

D 다음 괄호 안에서 알맞은 것을 고르시오.

1 The cake was sweet and (delicious / deliciously).

2 My friend is kind and (help / helpful).

3 He is both curious and (active / activity).

4 She spends her time reading novels and (watching / to watch) movies.

5 She smiled warmly and (bright / brightly).

6 He enjoys swimming and (run / running) in the morning.

7 She walked quickly and (quiet / quietly).

8 He is not only smart but also (creative / creativity).

9 He is neither lazy nor (careless / carelessly).

10 She is friendly and (honest / honestly).

11 She answered neither quickly nor (polite / politely).

12 My friend is smart and (kind / kindness) to everyone.

13 She promised to study hard and (help / helping) her friend.

14 She suggested either going shopping or (visit / visiting) a museum.

15 He is both a good speaker and (listens well / a good listener).

16 His hobby is drawing cartoons and (taking / to take) photos.

17 She agreed to join the club and (share / sharing) her ideas.

18 He admitted forgetting his homework and (lose / losing) his notebook.

19 We practiced writing essays and (speak / speaking) in English.

20 They decided to start the project and (finish / finishing) it on time.

 다음 대화의 괄호 안에서 알맞은 표현을 고르시오.

1   A: Did many people wait in front of the gate?

     B: At the gate (stood a long line of people / a long line of people stood).

2   A: Who came into the classroom just now?

     B: Into the classroom (came the teacher / the teacher came).

3   A: Where did the bus finally arrive?

     B: At the station (arrived the bus / the bus arrived).

4   A: Was the shop ever so crowded before?

     B: Rarely (the shop was / was the shop) busy.

5   A: Did the students ever speak so confidently?

     B: Hardly (they spoke / did they speak) with confidence.

6   A: Do you eat fast food very often?

     B: Never (I eat / do I eat) hamburgers and pizza these days.

7   A: Is he dealing with the situation well?

     B: Little (he understands / does he understand) what is really going on.

8   A: I am not very good at drawing pictures.

     B: Neither (am I / I am). I usually find it really difficult.

9   A: Does your mother cook delicious food?

     B: Yes, she does, and so (do / does) my grandmother.

10 A: Did the students understand the rule clearly?

     B: Yes, they did, and so (do / did) their parents.

A 다음 우리말에 맞는 강조 문장이 되도록 빈칸에 알맞은 단어를 쓰시오.

1 그들은 정말로 그 여행을 즐겼다.

→ They ___________ enjoy the trip.

2 그는 정말로 열심히 공부한다.

→ He ___________ study very hard.

3 나는 어제 그 소식을 확실히 들었다.

→ I ___________ hear the news yesterday.

4 그녀는 친구들을 정말로 많이 돕는다.

→ She ___________ help her friends a lot.

5 우리는 그 장면을 정말로 분명히 보았다.

→ We ___________ see that scene clearly.

6 학생들은 환경 문제에 정말로 관심이 있다.

→ The students ___________ care about environmental issues.

7 그녀는 지난주에 새 자전거를 정말로 샀다.

→ She ___________ buy a new bicycle last week.

8 나는 도서관에서 그녀를 정말로 우연히 만났다.

→ I ___________ meet her at the library by chance.

9 우리는 그 실험에서 정말로 놀라운 결과를 얻었다.

→ We ___________ get surprising results from the experiment.

10 나는 네가 말한 내용을 확실히 기억한다.

→ I ___________ remember what you said.

11 그들은 서로를 정말로 믿는다.

→ They ___________ trust each other.

12 우리는 그 문제를 정말로 완전히 해결했다.

→ We ___________ solve the problem completely.

1 나에게 조언을 해 준 것은 바로 부모님이었다.

→ It was my parents ___________ gave me advice.

2 나를 가장 걱정하게 만드는 것은 바로 이 문제이다.

→ ___________ is this problem that worries me the most.

3 우리를 행복하게 한 것은 바로 그의 노력이었다.

→ It was his effort ___________ made us happy.

4 우리가 시험을 치르는 날은 바로 내일이다.

→ ___________ is tomorrow that we have the exam.

5 우리가 사진을 찍은 곳은 바로 그 공원이었다.

→ It was in the park ___________ we took the photo.

6 네가 이 문제를 푸는 것이 중요하다.

→ It is important ___________ you to solve this problem.

7 그가 약속을 지킨 것은 현명했다.

→ It was wise ___________ him to keep the promise.

8 네가 늦게 도착한 것이 문제였다.

→ The problem was ___________ arriving late.

9 내가 일찍 일어나는 것은 쉽지 않다.

→ It isn't easy for ___________ to get up early.

10 우리는 그가 하루종일 불평하는 것에 질렸다.

→ We were tired of ___________ complaining all day.

11 그녀가 우산을 잊어버린 것이 문제였다.

→ The trouble was ___________ forgetting the umbrella.

12 우리가 사진을 너무 많이 찍은 것 때문에 핸드폰 배터리가 다 닳았다.

→ The phone battery died because of ___________ taking too many pictures.

C 다음 우리말에 맞도록 괄호 안의 단어들을 바르게 배열하시오.

1 나는 책을 읽고 음악을 듣는다.
(I / a book / and / music / read / listen to / .)

→ ____

2 그녀는 친절하지만 엄격하다.
(she / kind / but / is / strict / .)

→ ____

3 그는 침착하고 긍정적인 태도를 유지한다.
(stays / calm / positive / and / he / .)

→ ____

4 그는 열심히 공부하고 일한다.
(works / and / studies / hard / he / .)

→ ____

5 그녀는 여행을 하거나 사진을 찍기를 좋아한다.
(likes / or / to travel / she / take pictures / .)

→ ____

6 그는 운동을 하고 건강을 유지하려고 노력한다.
(he / stay healthy / to exercise / tries / and / .)

→ ____

7 그는 영어뿐만 아니라 프랑스어도 배운다.
(not only / he / learns / but also / English / French / .)

→ ____

8 나는 책을 읽을 뿐만 아니라 친구들과 토론도 한다.
(have discussions / not only / but also / books / read / with my friends / I / .)

→ ____

9 그녀는 강 옆에서와 숲속에서 사진을 찍었다.
(she / by the river / and / took / in the forest / photos / .)

→ ____

10 그 고양이는 소파 밑과 침대 위에서 잤다.
(the cat / and / on the bed / slept / under the sofa / .)

→ ____

D 다음 우리말에 맞도록 괄호 안의 단어들을 바르게 배열하시오.

1 나는 결코 만족하지 않았다. (was / satisfied / I)

→ Never ____.

2 그 방은 거의 조용하지 않았다. (was / quiet / the room)

→ Hardly ____.

3 그녀는 그 실수를 거의 알아차리지 못했다. (did / notice / she / the mistake)

→ Scarcely ____.

4 그녀는 거의 이해하지 못했다. (she / understand / did)

→ Little ____.

5 나는 그것을 거의 의심하지 않았다. (did / doubt / it / I)

→ Little ____.

6 그는 거의 집에 머무르지 않는다. (does / stay / he / at home)

→ Hardly ____.

7 그들은 좀처럼 그 계획에 동의하지 않는다. (do / they / the plan / on / agree)

→ Rarely ____.

8 그녀는 좀처럼 도움을 요청하지 않는다. (she / help / does / ask / for)

→ Seldom ____.

9 그녀는 영어로 거의 말할 수 없었다. (speak / could / she / English)

→ Rarely ____.

10 그는 결코 우리를 실망시키지 않을 것이다. (disappoint / us / he / will)

→ Never ____.

11 나는 영어를 좋아한다, 그리고 내 친구도 그렇다. (so / my friend / does)

→ I like English and, ____.

12 그녀는 피곤하지 않았다, 그리고 나도 피곤하지 않았다.
(neither / was / tired / and / I / she / not / was / ,)

→ ____.

1 다음 중 밑줄 친 부분이 어법상 <u>틀린</u> 것은?

① We <u>do appreciate</u> your help.

② He <u>does read</u> a lot of books.

③ I <u>did meet</u> her at the concert.

④ She <u>do studies</u> hard every night.

⑤ They <u>did enjoy</u> the trip to Jeju Island.

[2-4] 다음 중 빈칸에 들어갈 말로 가장 적절한 것을 고르시오.

2

I ________ remember locking the door.

① do　　　　② does

③ done　　　④ doing

⑤ to do

3

They ________ watch a movie together yesterday morning.

① do　　　　② does

③ did　　　　④ doing

⑤ done

4

It is her effort ________ makes the team successful.

① who　　　　② what

③ that　　　　④ when

⑤ where

[5-6] 다음 빈칸에 들어갈 말로 적절한 것을 <u>모두</u> 고르시오.

5

It is my sister ________ always supports me.

① what

② that

③ when

④ who

⑤ which

6

It was on the bench ________ they were sitting yesterday.

① who

② what

③ that

④ when

⑤ where

보기 of   for   us   we   her   she

7

초록불일 때 우리가 길을 건너는 것은 안전하다.

→ It is safe __________ us to cross the street when the light is green.

8

네가 친구를 비웃은 것은 무례했다.

→ It was rude __________ you to laugh at your friend.

9

우리가 그 새로운 카페를 찾는 것은 쉬웠다.

→ It was easy for __________ to find the new café.

10

우리는 그녀가 마라톤을 완주한 것에 감탄했다.

→ We admired __________ finishing the marathon.

[11-12] 다음 문장에서 어법상 틀린 곳을 찾아 바르게 고치시오.

11

She smiled warmly and gentle at the child.

__________________ → __________________

12

My hobby is playing games and watched movies.

__________________ → __________________

13 다음 글의 밑줄 친 부분 중 어법상 틀린 곳은?

Sarah ①does like playing the piano, so she practices every day. She often tells her friends that she ②does enjoy music more than anything else. Last week, she ③joined a music contest and won a prize. She believes it is her teacher ④who gave her confidence. After the contest, she said it was her effort ⑤what made the success possible.

①　　②　　③　　④　　⑤

[14-16] 다음 중 어법상 틀린 문장을 고르시오.

14

① On the hill stood an old house.

② In the corner was a small wooden box.

③ In the mountains were a quiet village.

④ Under the tree sat a little boy.

⑤ At the bus stop were many students.

15

① Never was the room so quiet.

② Hardly does he speak French.

③ Seldom does he forget his homework.

④ Little did I know about the plan.

⑤ Rarely the teacher was late for class.

16

① Seldom do students finish their exams early.

② Rarely do I agree to such an idea.

③ Little did she know what would happen next.

④ Never can machines completely replace humans.

⑤ Hardly did they noticed the danger ahead.

[17-19] 다음 우리말에 맞도록 괄호 안의 단어를 이용하여 빈칸에 알맞은 말을 쓰시오.

17

버스는 빙판길에서 천천히 그리고 안전하게 움직였다. (safe)

→ The bus moved slowly and ____________ on the icy road.

18

그들은 노래 부르기와 춤추기를 함께 연습했다. (dance)

→ They practiced singing and ____________ together.

19

축제에는 전통 춤을 공연하는 것뿐만 아니라 지역 음식을 나누는 것도 포함되었다. (share)

→ The festival included not only performing traditional dances but also ____________ local food.

20

A: I am really interested in science.
B: ______________________________.

① So am I
② So did I
③ So will I
④ Neither do I
⑤ No, I'm not

21

A: She studied hard for the test.
B: ______________________________.

① So will my brother
② So did my brother
③ So does my brother
④ Neither is my brother
⑤ Neither can my brother

22

A: We didn't watch the movie yesterday.
B: ______________________________.

① So did we
② Neither did we
③ So do we
④ Neither can we
⑤ So have we

23 다음 두 대화의 빈칸에 들어갈 말이 바르게 짝지어진 것은?

• A: Who helped you with the science project?
  B: It was my friend _________ gave me the best ideas.
• A: Was the place peaceful?
  B: No, never _________ quiet.

① what - was it
② which - was it
③ that - was it
④ that - it is
⑤ who - it was

24 다음 글의 밑줄 친 부분 중 어법상 옳은 것끼리 바르게 짝지어진 것은?

Last summer, I ⓐdid visit Canada with my family. We enjoyed traveling and ⓑlearn new cultures. At the museum, the guide spoke ⓒslowly and clearly. Seldom ⓓdid the night sky so beautiful in my life. It was so quiet outside. My parents didn't like crowded places, and ⓔneither did my brother.

① ⓐ, ⓑ
② ⓑ, ⓒ
③ ⓑ, ⓓ
④ ⓐ, ⓒ, ⓔ
⑤ ⓑ, ⓓ, ⓔ

혼공 중학 영문법 마스터

정답

CHAPTER 1
관계사 1

A 1 I know someone <u>who</u> helps others.
2 She found a letter <u>which</u> surprised her.
3 He has a friend <u>who</u> plays the piano well.

B 1 who 2 whose 3 that

C 1 that 2 what 3 what

D 1 I changed my phone <u>that</u> I bought last year.
2 He sold the computer <u>which</u> I wanted.
3 The girl <u>who is</u> singing at the concert is Anna.
4 The students <u>who are</u> studying are smart.

A 1 I know the boy <u>who</u> runs fast.
2 I saw the man <u>who</u> helps animals.
3 Amy is the girl <u>who</u> likes soccer.
4 You saw the movie <u>which</u> I like.
5 He talked to the man <u>whose</u> son is a doctor.
6 You helped the girl <u>whom</u> I taught.
7 She has friends <u>whose</u> cats are cute.
8 She walks the dog <u>that</u> can jump high.

B 1 who 2 that 3 that 4 who 5 whose
6 which 7 that 8 whose

C 1 who 2 which 3 whose 4 whose
5 which 6 which

D 1 what 2 what 3 that[which] 4 what
5 that[which] 6 what 7 that[which]
8 what

A 1 who 2 who 3 who 4 who 5 which
6 which 7 who 8 which 9 who
10 that 11 that 12 which 13 that
14 which 15 which 16 that 17 that
18 that 19 who 20 that

B 1 whose 2 whose 3 who 4 whose
5 which 6 whose 7 whose 8 who
9 whose 10 who 11 which 12 whose
13 which 14 whose 15 who 16 which
17 whose 18 whose 19 whose
20 whose

C 1 whom 2 which 3 which 4 whom
5 which 6 which 7 which 8 who
9 that 10 whom 11 that 12 that
13 that 14 that 15 which 16 that
17 which 18 that 19 which 20 which

D 1 what 2 what 3 that 4 what 5 that
6 what 7 what 8 that 9 what 10 that

A 1 which 2 who 3 who 4 whose 5 who
6 who 7 whose 8 who 9 whose
10 which 11 who 12 whose

B 1 who 2 which 3 which 4 who[whom]
5 which 6 which 7 which 8 which
9 who[whom] 10 which 11 which
12 who[whom]

C 1 I remember the girl who helped me.
2 She interviewed the player who kicks the ball.
3 I found the app which records sound.
4 I met a boy whose bike was stolen.
5 He installed the camera which detects movement.
6 I found the smartwatch whose battery was dead.
7 He is the leader whom everyone trusts.
8 She sent a letter to the friend whom I met.
9 We cleaned up the tools which we used.

10 He understood the rule that the teacher explained.

D 1 She sang the song that I like.
2 He regretted what he said.
3 Do you remember what I did?
4 I read the poem that he wrote.
5 You won't believe what I saw.
6 We followed what you showed.
7 I didn't know what she gave me.
8 I recorded what my friend played.
9 He bought everything that she wanted.
10 He deleted the email I sent.

혼공실전 ㅋ   pp. 20–23

1 ④ 2 ① 3 ② 4 which 5 who
6 whose 7 ①, ③ 8 ④ 9 ⑤
10 which → whose 11 whom → which[that]
12 ②

Mike는 전학 온 지 얼마 안 된 한 소년을 만났다. 그들은 수업이 아주 재미있었던 선생님에 대해 이야기했다. 그 소년은 Mike에게 영어 숙제를 도와주는 웹사이트를 보여 주었다. 이후 그들은 Mike가 과학 동아리에서 알게 된 한 여자아이와 함께 농구를 했다. 경기가 끝난 뒤, 그들은 떡볶이를 파는 분식집에 갔다.

13 ③ 14 ② 15 who[that] 16 which[that]
17 whose 18 what 19 ⑤ 20 ②
21 I read the book that you like. 22 ①
23 ④

나는 제주에 사는 사촌이 있다. 그는 바다에서 수영하기를 좋아하는 개를 키운다. 우리는 종종 해변 근처에 집이 있는 그 사촌을 방문한다. 우리는 쿠키가 맛있던 그의 누나에게 감사 인사를 했다. 그는 또 여행에 대해 자신이 쓴 책을 나에게 보여 주었다.

CHAPTER 2
관계사 2

혼공개념   pp. 26–27

A 1 We saw many paintings, <u>and they</u> impressed us.
2 He missed the bus, <u>and it</u> made him late for school.

B 1 when 2 where 3 why

C 1 Whoever 2 whichever 3 whatever

D 1 whenever 2 wherever 3 However

혼공연습   pp. 28–29

A 1 who 2 who 3 which 4 who 5 which
6 which 7 who 8 which

B 1 where 2 why 3 when 4 where
5 how 6 when 7 where 8 the way

C 1 Whoever 2 anything 3 Whoever
4 anything 5 anyone 6 anything

D 1 whenever 2 wherever 3 Whenever
4 Wherever 5 However

혼공실전 1   pp. 30–33

A 1 who 2 who 3 which 4 it 5 she
6 it 7 who 8 which 9 which 10 who
11 which 12 which 13 it 14 which
15 which 16 which 17 which 18 which
19 it 20 which

B 1 where 2 when 3 where 4 why
5 the way 6 the reason why 7 the place
8 the time 9 where 10 when
11 the way 12 when 13 where 14 why
15 when 16 when 17 where 18 where
19 when 20 where

Ĉ 1 Whoever 2 whatever 3 whichever
4 whoever 5 whatever 6 whichever
7 whichever 8 Whatever 9 who
10 Whoever 11 who 12 that 13 that
14 what 15 who 16 what 17 who
18 which 19 which 20 what

D̂ 1 wherever 2 whenever 3 whenever
4 wherever 5 at any time when
6 at any place where 7 when 8 where
9 where 10 how

Â 1 which 2 which 3 who 4 which
5 which 6 it 7 they 8 which 9 who
10 they 11 which 12 it

B̂ 1 where 2 when 3 where 4 why
5 when 6 where 7 when 8 place
9 why 10 where 11 time 12 way

Ĉ 1 He can make whatever you want.
2 You can choose whichever color you like.
3 Whoever makes me laugh can be my friend.
4 You can reserve whichever seat you want.
5 She took a picture of whatever I made.
6 Anyone who has a question must raise their hand.
7 I will read anything that you recommend.
8 I fixed anything that he broke.
9 No matter which bus you take, you can get to the city hall.
10 No matter what you choose, your family will support you.

D̂ 1 You can call me whenever you want.
2 They make friends wherever they go.
3 We greeted him whenever we saw him.
4 You can study English wherever you are.
5 He eats a snack at any time when he is hungry.
6 People gather at any place where he sings.
7 However you interpret it, the result is the same.

8 No matter when we leave, the arrival time is the same.
9 No matter where you are, I will find you.
10 No matter how I explain, he can't understand that.

1 ③, ④ 2 ③ 3 ② 4 ⑤ 5 ④ 6 ③
7 Whichever 8 Whoever 9 Anyone
10 why → who 11 Anything → Anyone
12 ④

Tom은 토요일에 공원에 갔다. 그는 함께 하기를 원하는 누구와도 축구를 했다. 경기가 끝난 후, 그는 간식을 나누어 주며 "네가 원하는 어떤 것이든 가져도 돼."라고 말했다. 그는 벤치에서 누가 자기 옆에 앉든 개의치 않았다. 친구들이 어떤 음료를 고르든, 그는 행복했다. 그는 모두를 웃게 하기 위해 자기가 가진 것은 무엇이든 내주었다.

13 ⑤ 14 ④ 15 when 16 wherever
17 However 18 ⑤ 19 I know the reason why he didn't attend the meeting.
20 No matter what you think, it's your choice.
21 ② 22 ② 23 ①

Semi는 친절한 학생이다. 누군가 도움이 필요할 때마다, 그녀는 늘 도울 준비가 되어 있다. 그녀가 어디를 가더라도, 그녀는 사람들을 행복하게 만든다. 사람들의 이야기가 아무리 길더라도, 그녀는 인내심 있게 듣는다. 무슨 일이 일어나더라도, 그녀는 침착하고 친절함을 유지한다. 그리고 상황이 아무리 힘들어져도, 그녀는 결코 포기하지 않는다.

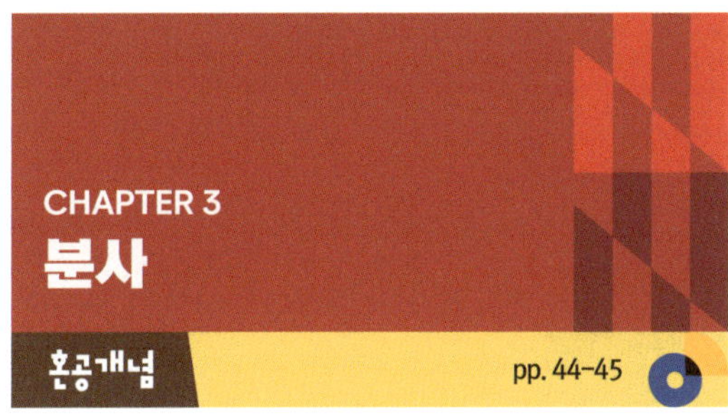

A 1 crying 2 broken 3 reading 4 baked

B 1 annoying 2 excited 3 interesting

C Born

D 1 Because, I, was 2 When, they

A 1 ○ 2 X 3 ○ 4 ○ 5 ○ 6 ○ 7 X
8 X

B 1 buzzing 2 stained 3 bored 4 broken
5 painted 6 running 7 yawning
8 boring

C 1 Smiling 2 Reading
3 Being 4 Having 5 It being

D 1 I finish 2 it was rainy 3 the lights went
4 the bell rang 5 I was cleaning[I cleaned]

A 1 △ 2 ○ 3 ○ 4 △ 5 ○ 6 X 7 ○
8 X 9 ○ 10 ○ 11 X 12 ○ 13 △
14 X 15 △ 16 X 17 X 18 ○ 19 △
20 ○

B 1 singing 2 flying 3 sealed 4 bent
5 playing 6 rolling 7 stuck 8 blown
9 rising 10 running 11 resting
12 barking 13 folded 14 blocked
15 meowing 16 crushed 17 cracked
18 laughing 19 jumping 20 damaged

C 1 interested, interested
2 bored, boring

3 annoyed, annoyed

4 frightened, frightening

5 interesting, interested

6 scratched, stuck

7 exciting, excited

8 depressed, depressing

9 surprising, surprised

10 disgusted, disgusting

D 1 Working hard
2 Though[Being] tired 3 Hurrying
4 Being sick 5 Having lost
6 Being exhausted 7 Opening 8 cooking
9 Liking 10 Jogging 11 Not studying
12 It getting

A 1 flying[fly] 2 lying[lie] 3 rolling
4 stretching[stretch] 5 torn 6 broken
7 turning 8 diving[dive] 9 waving
10 folded 11 damaged 12 swinging

B 1 painted 2 depressed 3 lying 4 closed
5 Cooking 6 waiting 7 Trapped
8 Satisfied 9 Exhausted 10 Surprised
11 Filled 12 eating

C 1 That buzzing sound is so annoying.
2 We saw a whispering boy.
[We saw a boy whispering.]
3 We washed the burned pan.
4 You watched the blinking light.
[You watched the light blinking.]
5 The puppy followed a creeping bug.
6 The boy sent a letter written in blue.
7 She sewed up the shirt torn by the fence.
8 They fixed the damaged window.
9 They felt excited before the game.
10 He found a poster attached to the wall.

D 1 Loving music, I joined the band.
2 (While) Walking, we saw a rainbow.
3 Not being ready, he made us wait.

4 Having finished, we can relax now.

5 Having forgotten his umbrella, he got wet.

6 The weather being bad, we stayed indoors.

7 When I turned around the corner, I saw a cat.

8 If you study, you will pass the exam.

9 When the movie ended, everyone clapped.

10 Because they were caught in the rain, they ran into a shop.

11 Because the building was ruined by the fire, it was rebuilt later.

12 Because the tower was built in 1887, it is a famous landmark.

1 ③　**2** ④　**3** ①, ③　**4** ②　**5** ④　**6** ④

7 ③　**8** boring　**9** depressed　**10** Walking

11 The light being　**12** ⑤　**13** ②, ④　**14** ③

15 ②　**16** shocking → shocked

17 Knowing → Known

18 The boy playing the guitar is my brother.

19 The book chosen for the contest was very thick.

20 When[As] the teacher entered

21 Because[As, Since] he was left alone

22 Frightened → Frightening　**23** ④

시원한 가을 바람을 즐기며, Sandra는 연못 근처 벤치에 앉았다. 갑자기, 산들바람이 불었고, 그녀는 나무에서 떨어지는 나뭇잎들을 보았다. 작은 아이를 품에 안은 채, 한 여성이 그녀 옆을 지나갔다.

자연에 둘러싸여, Sandra는 편안함을 느꼈다. 그녀는 자신의 공책을 꺼냈다. 평화로운 풍경에 영감을 받아, 그녀는 가을의 아름다움에 대한 시를 쓰기 시작했다.

CHAPTER 4
과거완료와 가정법

A **1** had fixed　**2** Had　**3** hadn't

B **1** studies, will　**2** were, could

C **1** 그녀가 더 일찍 출발했더라면, 버스를 탔을 텐데.
　2 내가 강했더라면, 그 상자를 들 수 있었을 텐데.

D **1** could pass　**2** were

A **1** had eaten　**2** had fed　**3** had bought
　4 had drawn　**5** had written
　6 had finished　**7** had studied
　8 had arrived

B **1** will　**2** uses　**3** call　**4** will remember
　5 would take　**6** would learn　**7** helped
　8 saved

C **1** had been　**2** had had　**3** had finished
　4 had taken　**5** had not snowed

D **1** lived　**2** had passed　**3** had taken
　4 were　**5** had won

A **1** Had　**2** has not arrived
　3 has never eaten　**4** had studied
　5 have lived　**6** have known　**7** had studied
　8 had packed　**9** Had　**10** Had
　11 had lost　**12** Had　**13** had read
　14 had opened　**15** had finished
　16 had drawn　**17** had cleaned
　18 had done　**19** had cooked
　20 had lived

B 1 don't 2 save 3 practices 4 wake
5 will 6 will 7 asked 8 ate 9 had
10 would 11 could 12 would

C 1 had not been 2 had taken 3 had worn
4 had not fallen 5 had done 6 had found
7 could have avoided 8 would have gone
9 would have told 10 could have been
11 would have failed
12 would not have been

D 1 had, could 2 were, didn't 3 had, had
4 had set, had set 5 had joined, had joined
6 were, knew 7 owned, had
8 didn't, talked 9 had been, stay
10 had walked, were

 **혼공실전 ㄹ** pp. 70-73

A 1 had washed 2 had eaten 3 had finished
4 had bought 5 hadn't packed 6 had lost
7 hadn't read 8 had missed
9 hadn't eaten 10 hadn't met
11 had practiced 12 had been stolen

B 1 were 2 were 3 knew 4 were
5 would 6 would 7 will 8 spend 9 save
10 avoid 11 took 12 would call 13 were
14 will 15 don't 16 will 17 will 18 joins
19 could 20 practices

C 1 ran → runs 2 woke → wakes
3 understood → will[can] understand
4 will → would 5 will → would
6 can → could 7 know → knew
8 have → had 9 have → had
10 watch → have watched 11 be → been
12 took → taken 13 have → had
14 know → known 15 will → would

D 1 I wish I could sing well.
2 I wish I were good at math.
3 I wish I had many friends.
4 I wish I didn't have homework.

5 I wish I had not lost my wallet.
6 They run as if they were athletes.
7 He dances as if he were on TV.
8 She sings as if she were a star.

E 1 내가 그 콘서트에 갔었더라면 좋을 텐데.
2 그는 그 게임을 마치 진짜인 것처럼 한다.
3 내가 사진을 많이 찍었더라면 좋을 텐데.
4 내가 그렇게 많이 먹지 않았었더라면 좋을 텐데.
5 그녀는 마치 아무 걱정도 없는 것처럼 웃는다.

 **혼공실전 ㅋ** pp. 74-77

1 ⑤ 2 ⑤ 3 ③ 4 ④ 5 had left
6 as if 7 ⑤ 8 ② 9 ⑤ 10 ④
11 played → had played
12 have → had
13 wouldn't have 14 been, have
15 had 16 Jim talks as if he had read the book.
17 Katie sings as if she had taken lessons.
18 we had PE class today
19 I had brought my umbrella
20 will → would 21 am → were 22 ②, ④
23 ③

우리는 지난 겨울 파리에 가지 않았다. 우리가 거기에
갔더라면 좋았을 것이다. 내 친구는 마치 파리에 갔었던
것처럼 말하지만, 실제로는 가지 않았다. 우리가 파리에
있었더라면, 에펠탑을 볼 수 있었을 것이다. 내가 만약
부자라면, 언젠가 세계를 여행할 것이다.

CHAPTER 5
접속사
혼공개념
pp. 80–81

A 1 I heard <u>that you moved to a new school.</u>
2 <u>Whether you join us or not</u> is your choice.

B 1 after 2 Although

C 1 and 2 or 3 also

D 1 However 2 Nevertheless

혼공연습
pp. 82–83

A 1 주어 2 목적어 3 보어 4 보어 5 주어
6 보어 7 목적어 8 보어

B 1 When 2 While 3 Before 4 Because
5 Although

C 1 and 2 or 3 nor 4 also 5 or 6 nor
7 and 8 also

D 1 However 2 Therefore 3 Nevertheless
4 For example 5 Likewise

혼공실전 1
pp. 84–87

A 1 that 2 that 3 whether 4 that 5 that
6 that 7 whether 8 That 9 that
10 that 11 that 12 if 13 That
14 Whether 15 that 16 whether
17 Whether 18 if 19 that 20 whether

B 1 While 2 As 3 After 4 Because
5 Although 6 Even though 7 Before
8 While 9 Although 10 Even though
11 When 12 After 13 so that
14 Even if 15 that

C 1 and 2 or 3 nor 4 also 5 and
6 or 7 nor 8 only 9 Both 10 both

11 either 12 neither 13 but 14 or
15 Neither 16 but 17 both 18 or
19 nor 20 only

D 1 However 2 Therefore 3 Moreover
4 Thus 5 Nevertheless 6 For example
7 Furthermore 8 As a result 9 By the way

혼공실전 2
pp. 88–91

A 1 that 2 that 3 if[whether]
4 if[whether] 5 that 6 that 7 that
8 if[whether] 9 that 10 that 11 that
12 if[whether]

B 1 When 2 While 3 Before 4 Because
5 so that 6 Although 7 after 8 Because
9 Although 10 When 11 Although
12 so that

C 1 She can speak both English and Japanese.
2 You can take either the bus or the subway.
3 He is neither a good swimmer nor a good
runner.
4 He is not only kind but also smart.
5 He wants either the pizza or the hamburger.
6 She not only sings but also dances.
7 I like neither the movie nor the book.
8 I respect both my math teacher and my
English teacher.
9 She can not only paint but also sing.
10 You can order either a salad or soup.

D 1 I studied hard. However, the test was difficult.
2 It rained a lot. As a result, the game was
canceled.
3 The book is interesting. Moreover, it is useful.
4 He was tired. Nevertheless, he kept running.
5 He always practiced. Therefore, he won
the contest.
6 The weather is nice. By the way, what are
your plans?
7 He finished his homework. Besides, he
also cleaned the room.

8 The bus was delayed. Thus, we were late.

9 His room is clean. In contrast, his brother's room is messy.

10 He regularly exercised.[He exercised regularly.] As a result, his health improved.

1 ④　2 ⑤　3 ④　4 ①　5 ⑤　6 ④

7 and　8 nor　9 but　10 nor → or

11 not → but　12 ④

Sarah는 일에서 벗어나 휴식을 취하고 싶어서 산으로 캠핑을 갔다. 그녀는 해가 지기 전에 돌아올 것이라고 생각했다. 산책로를 따라 걷는 동안, 그녀는 새들이 지저귀는 소리를 즐겼다. 캠핑장에 도착하자, 그녀는 강가에 있는 자리나 큰 참나무 아래에 있는 자리 중 하나를 선택할 수 있었다. 비록 비가 내리기 시작했지만, 그녀는 계속 있기로 결정했다.

13 ⑤　14 ①　15 that　16 so that

17 nor　18 ②

19 I read not only books but also magazines.

20 We should protect the environment. For instance, we can recycle plastic.　21 ③

22 ④　23 ③

1. Hana는 그림 그리기를 좋아한다. 비슷하게, 그녀는 종종 너무 바쁘다.
2. 그녀는 학교에서 열심히 공부한다. 게다가, 그녀는 친구들이 영어 공부하는 것을 도와준다.
3. 그녀는 더 나은 성적을 원했다. 그럼에도 불구하고, 매일 밤 공부했다.
4. 그녀는 동물을 좋아한다. 예를 들어, 그녀는 개를 돌본다.
5. 그녀는 반 친구들에게 친절하다. 대조적으로, 그들은 그녀에게 친절하다.

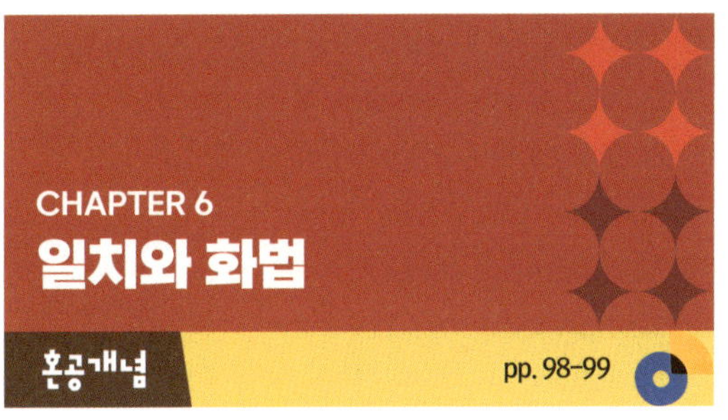

CHAPTER 6
일치와 화법

A　1 runs　2 are　3 are

B　1 ②　2 ③

C　1 he　2 could

D　1 asked　2 who the man is

A　1 ○　2 ✕　3 ✕　4 ✕　5 ○　6 ○　7 ✕
8 ✕　9 ✕　10 ✕

B　1 ✕　2 ○　3 ✕　4 ○　5 ✕　6 ○　7 ✕
8 ○　9 ○　10 ✕

C　1 he　2 had to　3 he was　4 would go
5 had seen

D　1 to　2 if[whether] I　3 told, to
4 what I was　5 how I solved　6 I would be

A　1 is　2 is　3 was　4 are　5 have　6 has
7 makes　8 helps　9 is　10 is　11 enjoy
12 are　13 have　14 support　15 are
16 grow　17 support　18 was　19 howl
20 performs

B　1 was　2 is studying　3 had lost　4 live
5 was cooking　6 will rain　7 doesn't like
8 had broken　9 hadn't seen　10 was
11 had just finished　12 goes

C　1 was　2 could　3 they　4 at that time
5 he, his　6 the next day　7 had seen
8 that day　9 I have　10 can run　11 I can
12 I will

D 1 I went 2 to clean 3 I liked 4 he was
5 told 6 the cat was 7 to close
8 if[whether] she will come 9 to me
10 what this word means
11 when the concert will start
12 how long they will stay
13 where my umbrella is 14 what he said
15 how tall she is

A 1 is → are 2 come → comes
3 passes → pass 4 are → is
5 make → makes 6 is → are
7 keep → keeps 8 don't → doesn't
9 smell → smells 10 are → is 11 is → are
12 are → is 13 are → is 14 agrees → agree
15 are → is

B 1 had been 2 will leave
3 had arrived 4 had read 5 is
6 had bought 7 are 8 was
9 had forgotten 10 plays 11 runs
12 had gone

C 1 James said that he was busy.
2 Emma said that she had to go home.
3 Mia said that she had a new phone.
4 Tom said that he could play the guitar.
5 Ben said that he would go to the library.
6 Mike said that he was going to school.
7 Jack said that he was playing soccer.
8 Lucy said that she was sleepy at that time.
9 Olivia said that she could finish it that day.
10 Henry said that he would see her the
   next day.
11 Daniel said that he had finished his lunch.
12 Minho said that he had watched TV the
   day before.

D 1 He asked where I was going.
2 She asked who closed the door.
3 He asked when I had arrived.

4 She asked if I could carry the bag.
5 Do you know where he is?
6 Do you know when I get up?
7 Can you tell me how tall she is?
8 Do you know why she is angry?
9 I wonder how this app works.
10 Do you know where the restaurant is?

1 ② 2 ③ 3 ② 4 ④ 5 ① 6 ⑤
7 if[whether] I had finished 8 to be
9 ③ 10 One, plays 11 where she lived
12 ③ 13 ④ 14 are → is 15 was → were
16 Tell me where he is.
17 I wonder how he learned to speak English.
18 ② 19 ② 20 will → would
21 lives → live / are → is 22 ②, ④ 23 ③

　　Jane과 Daniel은 오후 3시에 카페에서 만나기로 했
다. 이미 거의 4시가 되었지만 Daniel은 아직 오지 않았
다. 그녀는 그가 버스를 놓쳤는지 아니면 무슨 일이 일어
났는지 궁금해했다. 그녀는 왜 그가 늦는지 알지 못했다.
10분을 더 기다린 후, 그녀는 마침내 숨을 헐떡이며 카
페 쪽으로 달려오는 Daniel을 보았다. 그는 사과하며 버
스가 고장났었다고 설명했다.

CHAPTER 7
비교

 pp. 116–117 

A 1 faster 2 nicest 3 happier 4 most

B 1 big 2 fast 3 long

C 1 cleaner 2 than 3 the easier

D 1 She is the tallest student in the class.
   2 This is the best cake I have ever eaten.

혼공연습 pp. 118–119

A 1 ○ 2 ○ 3 X 4 ○ 5 ○ 6 ○ 7 X
   8 ○ 9 X 10 ○ 11 ○ 12 X 13 ○
   14 ○ 15 X

B 1 as tall as 2 Mia, Kim 3 as big as
   4 not, as fast 5 twice as tall

C 1 faster 2 cheaper 3 younger 4 cold
   5 wide 6 heavier 7 interesting
   8 comfortable 9 eldest 10 quickest

D 1 longer 2 much 3 more slowly
   4 fastest 5 least 6 less

혼공실전 1 pp. 120–123

A 1 kinder, kindest
   2 larger, largest
   3 closer, closest
   4 fatter, fattest
   5 sadder, saddest
   6 luckier, luckiest
   7 prettier, prettiest
   8 earlier, earliest
   9 better, best
   10 worse, worst
   11 more, most

12 less, least
13 farther[further], farthest[furthest]
14 cleverer, cleverest
15 narrower, narrowest
16 simpler, simplest
17 brighter, brightest
18 lower, lowest
19 more famous, most famous
20 more comfortable, most comfortable

B 1 X 2 X 3 ○ 4 ○ 5 ○ 6 X 7 ○
   8 X 9 ○ 10 X 11 ○ 12 ○ 13 ○
   14 ○ 15 ○ 16 ○ 17 X 18 X 19 X
   20 ○

C 1 tall 2 faster 3 sunnier 4 wide
   5 than 6 than 7 as 8 than 9 as
   10 than 11 clearer 12 new 13 easier
   14 narrower 15 warmer 16 honestly
   17 beautiful 18 crowded 19 big as
   20 cheaper

D 1 messier 2 bigger 3 softest 4 oldest
   5 slowly 6 most honest 7 happiest
   8 biggest 9 expensive 10 greatest
   11 sweeter 12 most peaceful
   13 funniest 14 quieter 15 longest
   16 much 17 most generous
   18 most interesting 19 cleaner
   20 better

혼공실전 2 pp. 124–127 

A 1 as bright as 2 as sweet as 3 as high as
   4 as loud as 5 as blue as 6 as long as
   7 as easy as 8 as light as 9 as strong as
   10 as loudly as possible[as loudly as he could]
   11 as far as possible[as far as she could]
   12 as much as possible[as much as I can]

B 1 not as[so] fast as 2 not as[so] deep as
   3 not as[so] fresh as 4 not as[so] heavy as
   5 twice as fast as 6 three times as long as
   7 brighter than 8 safer than

9 juicier than   10 funnier than

11 more crowded than

12 friendlier[more friendly] than

C 1 He jumped as high as possible.

2 My glass is not as full as yours.

3 The tower is taller than the trees.

4 The road is smoother than before.

5 These shoes are more expensive than the old jacket.

6 The old coins are as valuable as gold.

7 My shirt is cleaner than my pants.

8 The weather is cooler than last week.

9 Her scores were better than average.

10 The waves are stronger than yesterday.

11 The painting is not as vivid as the photos.

12 Team sports are more exciting than golf.

D 1 wider, as wide

2 heavier, as heavy

3 faster, much

4 deeper, as deep

5 cheap, even

6 funny, funniest

7 easy, easiest

8 exciting, most exciting

9 inspiring, most inspiring

10 memorable, most memorable

1 ③ 2 ③ 3 ⑤ 4 ③ 5 ④ 6 ③ 7 ②

8 ② 9 as, as possible   10 not as[so], as

11 times as, as   12 Emma is not as tall as John.

13 The rabbit is much smaller than the pig.

14 Vivian is the shortest girl.   15 ⑤

16 ③, ⑤   17 easy → easily   18 bigger → big

19 the more I understand

20 are using cash less and less.   21 ④

22 ①, ③, ⑤   23 ②

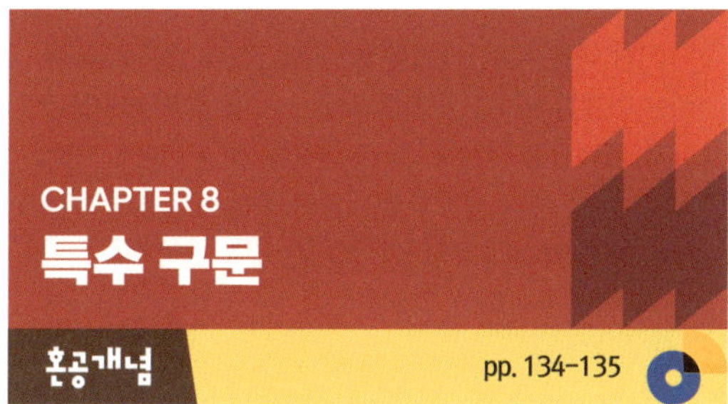

CHAPTER 8
특수 구문

A 1 did 2 does 3 that

B 1 It is important <u>for you</u> to study hard.
2 It was rude <u>of Sam</u> to speak like that.
3 I heard about <u>Sujin's</u> joining the soccer team.

C 1 intelligent 2 playing 3 practicing

D 1 sat two children 2 was the town
3 does

A 1 do 2 did 3 does 4 do 5 did 6 does
7 do 8 does

B 1 It is <u>Tom</u> that won the prize.
2 It was <u>my friend</u> who helped me.
3 It is <u>this book</u> that I want.
4 It was <u>her voice</u> that surprised me.
5 It is <u>at school</u> that we meet.
6 It is <u>on the beach</u> that we take a walk in summer.
7 It is <u>today</u> that we start the project.

C 1 It was difficult <u>for him</u> to carry the heavy box.
2 It was kind <u>of her</u> to share her lunch.
3 We were surprised at <u>their</u> winning the game.
4 It was wise <u>of him</u> to save money regularly.
5 It was foolish <u>of her</u> to believe that story.

D 1 seen 2 sees 3 see 4 saw 5 seeing

E 1 was the fishing boat
2 was the room 3 will they forget
4 do they know 5 is her sister 6 did I
7 stood the singer 8 have I seen
9 does he complain 10 is she

A 1 do 2 do 3 did 4 do 5 do 6 does
7 did 8 does 9 does 10 does 11 do
12 does 13 does 14 did 15 like
16 enjoy 17 hear 18 see 19 need
20 make

B 1 that 2 who 3 that 4 when 5 who
6 which 7 which 8 when 9 that
10 that

C 1 for you 2 of him 3 us 4 of her
5 them 6 for children 7 your 8 him
9 her 10 me

D 1 delicious 2 helpful 3 active
4 watching 5 brightly 6 running
7 quietly 8 creative 9 careless
10 honest 11 politely 12 kind 13 help
14 visiting 15 a good listener 16 taking
17 share 18 losing 19 speaking
20 finish

E 1 stood a long line of people
2 came the teacher 3 arrived the bus
4 was the shop 5 did they speak
6 do I eat 7 does he understand 8 am I
9 does 10 did

A 1 did 2 does 3 did 4 does 5 did
6 do 7 did 8 did 9 did 10 do 11 do
12 did

B 1 who[that] 2 It 3 that[which] 4 It
5 where[that] 6 for 7 of 8 your[you]
9 me 10 his[him] 11 her 12 our[us]

C 1 I read a book and listen to music.
2 She is kind but strict.
3 He stays calm and positive.
4 He studies and works hard.
5 She likes to travel or take pictures.

6 He tries to exercise and stay healthy.

7 He learns not only English but also French.

8 I not only read books but also have discussions with my friends.

9 She took photos by the river and in the forest.

10 The cat slept under the sofa and on the bed.

D 1 was I satisfied

2 was the room quiet

3 did she notice the mistake

4 did she understand

5 did I doubt it

6 does he stay at home

7 do they agree on the plan

8 does she ask for help

9 could she speak English

10 will he disappoint us

11 so does my friend

12 She was not tired, and neither was I

1 ④ 2 ① 3 ③ 4 ③ 5 ②, ④ 6 ③, ⑤

7 for 8 of 9 us 10 her

11 gentle → gently 12 watched → watching

13 ⑤

지난 여름, 나는 가족과 함께 캐나다를 방문했다. 우리는 여행과 새로운 문화를 배우는 것을 즐겼다. 박물관에서, 가이드는 천천히 그리고 분명하게 말했다. 내 인생에서 밤하늘이 그렇게 아름다웠던 적은 드물었다. 밖은 매우 조용했다. 내 부모님은 붐비는 곳을 좋아하지 않고, 내 남동생도 마찬가지였다.

Sarah는 피아노를 연주하는 것을 정말로 좋아해서, 매일 연습한다. 그녀는 종종 친구들에게 자신은 정말로 음악을 무엇보다 즐긴다고 말한다. 지난주에 그녀는 음악 경연 대회에 참가해서 상을 받았다. 그녀는 자신에게 자신감을 준 사람이 바로 선생님이라고 믿는다. 대회가 끝난 후, 그녀는 성공을 가능하게 한 것은 바로 자신의 노력이라고 말했다.

14 ③ 15 ⑤ 16 ⑤

17 safely 18 dancing 19 sharing

20 ① 21 ② 22 ② 23 ③ 24 ④

MEMO

혼공
중학 영문법
마스터
Level·3

초판 1쇄 발행   2026년 1월 19일

지은이   허준석
편집   김지혜 홍하늘 강지희
디자인   박새롬
마케팅   두잉글 사업본부

펴낸곳   혼공북스
출판등록   제2021-000288호
주소   04033 서울특별시 마포구 양화로 113, 4층(서교동, 순흥빌딩)
전자메일   team@hongong.co.kr

혼공북스는 ㈜혼공유니버스의 출판 브랜드입니다.

ISBN   979-11-984935-9-0   13740